NOT FEATHERS YET

A Beginner's Guide
to the Poetic Life

NOT FEATHERS YET

A Beginner's Guide
to the Poetic Life

Lola Haskins

Lola Haskins

The Backwaters Press

First Printing, April, 2007

Published by   The Backwaters Press
                3502 North 52nd Street
                Omaha, Nebraska 68104-3506

                gkosmicki@cox.net
                www.thebackwaterspress.homestead.com

ISBN: 0-9785782-6-0

TABLE OF CONTENTS

Preface

SECTION ONE: PRACTICALITIES

SECTION TWO: CONSIDERATIONS

Epilogue

NOT FEATHERS YET

A Beginner's Guide
to the Poetic Life

HOW TO USE THIS BOOK

Maybe you went out and bought this book yourself. Maybe someone bought it for you. Either way, someone, maybe it's you, thinks you're interested in poetry. But before I tell you what I hope we can do together, take a deep breath and walk over to the nearest window. Now, drop any pressure you may have been putting on yourself right out. Here are some thoughts beginning, and not-so-beginning, poets often hold in their heart of hearts: "If I'm going to write seriously, I'll need to publish sooner or later, or I won't have been successful." "I have the obligation to say something worth hearing every time I open my poetic mouth." "I'm pretty sure I'm not very good at this, so I don't have the right to claim I write poetry in the first place." Well, as they said in Donnie Brasco, "fa-ged about it!"—and for a very practical reason. Whether you're seventeen or fifty-seven, life is short. If you'll redirect the energy you spend worrying about publishing or being world-class to the job of playing, you'll find yourself with lots of starts at poems. Then, the real fun—after all, poems are mystery trips—begins. Some day, when you've accumulated enough poems you're happy with, you may want to collect them. Then you'll be in for different fun, because in putting a book together, you'll be learning a whole different mindset from the one that wrote the poems in the first place. That's because when you write poems, you have to think very small. But when you arrange them, you have to think globally, because a book's a process of which the poems are just the beginning, the way the stitches are the beginning of tapestries or motifs of symphonies. In other words, a really fine book of poems is always more than the sum of its parts. Playing, sharpening, and collecting—we'll be talking about all of that, and more.

But before we get started, let me make this clear. What I'm trying to do here is to help you learn to think like a poet. I'm also going to be giving you some practical advice (about publishing, reading, etc.) in case you decide you want to share your work with other people. But I'm not going to be talking much about technique. The poetic forms, the possibilities of enjambment, the implications of using certain vowels, the fine points of simile and metaphor—all these things are important, but they're the subject of another book.

What I want this one to be is a philosophy, a way to know what to do with the more technical books you may want, also, to buy. I think you may need this one first, because poetry texts and even books of exercises often assume you know some things which, personally, I didn't know when I started, maybe because I never formally studied writing, but maybe not. Besides, keep in mind that anything you learn—and here it's how to access your poetic self—is bound to feed into everything else you know, so that whereas on the surface this is a book about poetry, it is, like all books, really about life.

Here's the payoff. If what I hope happens for you, does, when you've been at this awhile you'll start feeling the kind of sensitization you get when someone's been stroking your skin. You'll start to notice things you'd have walked right by a few months ago—how your mailbox has turned into a bird with a yellow wing, how the sky's raining seeds, how that flock of leaves turns out to have been wrens— and pretty soon the world you thought you knew will seem unfamiliar, even if you never leave your street. In other words, if you can learn to look at and not past, if you never miss a chance to ask yourself, "What's this like?" then you won't wake up one morning and think, "Where was I all those years?" And, sure, it would be great if along the way you write some wonderful poems. But, you know, writing poetry is like going fishing. Whether you bring fish home or not (and fly fishermen understand this best), you'll have spent your day well and happily anyhow, just being by the river.

Before I finish, let me say a few words to you experienced writers. This book is pitched for beginners, because we're all beginners…and though it's true that much of it is my take on both the writing/life questions, and the practical things I wanted to know when I started out as a non-student adult, with no one to ask, I've also included topics which I hope will be of interest to those of you who long ago passed the stage we conventionally call "beginning."Try the chapters on putting a book together ("Orchestrating a Collection"), on giving a good reading ("Out Loud"), how to find good help ("Other People"), and the pros and cons of sticking to one poetic voice ("Elephants"). Maybe you'll even find something you didn't know in the rest. I hope so, because I see us—beginners, those of us who have made poetry our life's work, and everyone in between—not as a hierarchy, but as a community. Happy reading.

SECTION ONE

PRACTICALITIES

CHAPTER

1

GETTING STARTED

In this chapter, we're going to talk about how you can come up with the raw material from which you can make poems. But I'm not going to start, as you might think I would, with you or me sitting at a desk staring at a blank sheet of paper, and that's because what you need to understand is that being a poet isn't just who you are when you're at your desk. It's who you are all the time. Being a poet is a way of living in the world.

A lot of books on writing make a big point of telling you that you need to write every day. I agree that practice is important. I also agree that it's a good thing to get your pen (or fingers) flowing on a regular basis, but I don't think writing every day is necessarily what poets, as opposed to prose writers, should do, and popular as they are, morning pages (a.k.a. journaling) didn't work for me. When, for whatever reason, I'd miss a day or two, I used to flash back to the afternoon my dentist, who'd just finished propping my mouth with wads of cotton, was leaning over me saying, "You mean you don't floss every day?" And there I was sitting in that chair, seeing my pinkly gaping mouth with all its fake-silver imperfections reflected in her glasses, wanting never to go back to the dentist. But, truth in advertising: when I did journal, once in a while I'd come up with an image I could use. But since almost everything I wrote was petty, I felt I'd have been better off spending that time doing exercises. Now I know that some people write gorgeous and useful journals, and if keeping one works for you, do it.

Still, what I'm getting at is what I started with. In the long haul, just sitting down won't save you, because I don't think you can successfully be a poet unless you teach yourself how to be present as the world happens around you. Here's what I mean by that. Most of the time, we live on autopilot. We do what's on the list and go on. And we don't really look at the objects around us. Instead, we settle for the names we've been told they have. But poets don't operate like that. Poets are always looking, even when they aren't writing—into a shop window, say, at a box of candy, with its gold-foiled sweets spilling out onto red tiles, thinking, "H-m-m, what's this like?" or, alternatively, "What's this thinking?"

Let me give you an example. When I was out running this morning, I happened to notice the roadside ditches where some lupins were putting up their final stalks, and I thought, "Those look like candles." Then I thought about how candles burn to nubs, the way those yellow flowers are going to disappear. All that made me think of eternity, and eternity made me think of church. So when I opened my eyes back up, what I saw instead of lupins was aisles lined with candles. Then it was twilight in my mind and the way ahead was lined with soft glows.

Later on I noticed that the sun, which was now full up behind me, was elongating my shadow legs to the point where it looked like I was trying to run on stilts. Which made me think about vulnerability, how we colts teeter on unexpectedly long limbs we didn't know we were going to have, how at any moment we may fall.

I'm sure you get the idea. What you want to do is to be as present in your life as you can, and the way to do that is to notice the detail around you. I don't mean you should pursue this approach to the point of idiocy. Obviously we all have to live in the real world, and no matter what imagery I've been obsessing about for the past few hours, I still have to walk into the classroom. And when I'm in a car, I still need not to get distracted because a semi, icehouse or not, can still crush me, and great metaphorist or not, I'll still be dead.

Here's the bottom line. To deepen your existence in the world, all you have to do is look around the room you're in right now. Eventually, you'll catch on to the fact that nothing in it has only one name. Once you've figured that out, it's impossible to be bored, because something is always scurrying around below the surface—the way the pots that live under your counters have families, the way dramas happen in the folds of your curtains. Besides, and you'll have seen this by now too, if you try to think like that as you go, by the time you get to the blank page, it won't really be blank.

PLACE

Let's talk practicalities. First of all, if you're like me, it will help you get your mind in gear if you set up a designated writing place—

I've had everything from closets to a whole room—somewhere you can leave things spread out, somewhere where poetry's what you do when you go there. Otherwise, you'll always be tempted when nothing is coming into your head at the moment to switch your attention to something else. Ideally, it's good if your space is away from the public part of your house/apartment, because if it isn't, you'll be perpetually vulnerable to all the things that need doing, like studying, dusting, laundry, changing the oil in your car, etc. and you really should call Aunt So-and-So, and, oh my God, it's Susie's birthday, and barring those thoughts, there's always that phone bill you left sitting on the counter. I can be the woman of a thousand excuses when it suits me. So can you, so don't put yourself in that position if there's any way to avoid it.

While I'm on the subject, let me mention the Internet. There's something about e-mail that feels like dialing for dollars. Somewhere in our right brains, most of us believe that someone more legitimate than that oil-rich Nigerian might really be looking for us right now, maybe even the Nobel Prize committee. So if you write on a computer and it's hooked to the net, when you get stuck, you'll be tempted to check your mail. You'll swear you'll be on it that just for a minute, maybe five at the most. But once you give in to that impulse, it's never five minutes, not even close. Trust me, I know. So if this sounds familiar, you need to take your laptop away from anywhere that can take you away from your laptop.

Time

You'll remember that I said that the common prescription of writing every day may not apply to poets. But (and this is a large, non-anatomical "but") I'm convinced that if you're serious about writing, poetry or not, you're going to have to commit time to it on a regular basis or it just won't happen. How much time is, obviously, going to depend upon what other commitments you have. The main thing to keep in mind is that setting up blocks of time for writing and sticking to them is going to be crucial to long-term success. Because no matter how much we wish it did, poetry doesn't happen by thunderbolt, so if you're going to come up with raw material, especially the kind that develops into poems you'll want to keep, you'll need discipline. Besides, when that great wave does come along, it won't do you any good if you aren't at the beach. Give it some thought. Maybe you can put in a couple of hours late or early, when everyone else is asleep. Maybe you can pick certain days or parts of days. I was lucky that way because I taught Computer Science at a university, so I could I set two whole days aside—Tuesdays and Thursdays—since my classes met Monday, Wednesday, Friday.

Once you have your poetry time decided, it's crucial you don't let anyone preempt it by giving you errands to run or pressuring you to make the children's lunches since you're up early. Stick to your guns. These are your work hours and as important as what you get paid for.

TOOLS

Now you have a place and time, the implement(s) you use are obviously and absolutely of your choice. We're all different that way. Since I write as if I were improvising on a piano, I can't think without a keyboard. I've been hooked on keyboards since high school, when I started composing my papers on a typewriter. As an adult, I liked Underwoods, because they felt so solid—even though they were old-fashioned even then, even though their keys often stuck because my mind would move faster than my fingers. When I was in my late thirties I switched to IBM Selectrics, but reluctantly and only because I couldn't find another Underwood after my last one broke. Finally, partly goaded from the outside (you still write on WHAT?!), I started working on a computer. I hadn't thought I'd like that because screens remind me of TV. But now I can't imagine going back to the time when I couldn't move things around without retyping them. But that's just me. Some of my friends write everything by hand on yellow pads and go to the computer only when they're ready to edit; others write whole poems in their heads before they pick anything up. I wish I were like either group, because truly, if I don't have a keyboard handy, I'm handicapped.

I think I like keyboarding so much because it makes me feel physically freer than if I were clutching a pencil, and also because printed letters feel less personal to me than handwriting, so I tighten up less when I'm making them. But there's nothing objective about any of this. Go find your own idiosyncratic star. Use a particular color of paper, use only Macs, use only Eberhard Faber number 2s, use a purple flow-pen. Who cares? The point is to go with whatever makes you feel least encumbered.

No matter what you settle on, it's worth thinking about it that if you're stuck, switching methods can sometimes jump-start you. If you're using a keyboard, try paper. If you always write with your right hand, try your left. I admit that once in a blue moon, even I have come up with a line using an Eberhard Faber yellow pencil, a trick, which to me is very little short of magic.

ON IMPROV

You've arrived at your computer or your pad. You're sitting down. And? Well, if you have something started, of course you can work on that. But if you don't, then here's what to do. You want to let whatever may be hanging around in your fingers out, and you want to keep that process going for as long as you can. And during that time, whatever you do, don't think, especially not about where all this is going, if anywhere. Just keep typing.

Because you want to unhinge, you want to go back to being a kid concentrating so hard the corner of her tongue pokes out one side of her mouth. This kid is sprawled on the floor on a Sunday afternoon, scribbling on a pad, making lines so deep they groove the page. Sometimes she changes colors. Sometimes her pictures look like something and sometimes they don't. She just likes doing it. She doesn't ask herself if she's wasting her time. She doesn't ask her mother's opinion. She just looks through the box and picks up another crayon.

Now, that kid is my mentor and should be yours, because getting raw material on paper is all about getting back to being little, to seeing things freshly. There are great fringe benefits to being a kid when you're also an adult. To start with, you're going to have more fun than other people because as an adult you'll know that you haven't actually been everywhere and seen everything, so that teen- and mid-life everything-is-dull-and-boring monster can't get its hooks into you. Also, when you learn to kind of squint as you write, the way a kid squints to slide what she's seeing out of focus, all those things you've been noticing without knowing it will creep in under your fingers.

Of course, once the spate under your fingers stops, you're going to have to look at what you've written down. When you do, don't expect coherence, and don't expect a lot of great stuff. Out of all the lines of approach you've taken, there may be, if you're lucky, one or two you can use. If there's nothing this time, don't take it to heart. It just means that you needed to unload some lesser images so you could get to the good ones. It's like trying to find a particular scarf. You may have to pull all the other scarves in the drawer out to get at the one you want, which means, at the very least, that the floor will turn into your own personal landscape of mauve silk mountains and pale valleys. And if you're lucky, in the end you'll find yourself with the perfect scarf, draped like a negligee over your fingertips. Now if you're a guy, scarf searches may sound a little foreign, so try this on instead. You know when you're looking for, say, a crescent wrench, in that cobweb-draped tool chest in your shed, the one your girlfriend/wife/partner keeps nagging you to organize? Picture a little city of tools all over the floor as you plow through the drawers for the crescent wrench, which, inexplicably, you stuck in the miscellaneous-drill-bits drawer.

USING EXERCISES

In other words, getting anyplace often takes digging—not a problem. But sometimes it happens that you get to the bottom of your tool chest/drawer without finding anything useful. In that case, you might try an exercise, maybe one of the ones I've listed at the end of this chapter. And don't worry. Starting with an exercise lots of people have already used won't turn your poem into a clone of anyone's. If you begin with exactly the same image as every writer in the world who's sitting down right now, not even that would matter, because most free-writing, maybe even most writing, is a variation on a Rorschach test, in which ten people looking at an inkblot will report ten different interpretations. And why? Because each viewer brings her specific life to it in her hands, cupped as if she were about to take a drink, and sees her own face reflected every time she looks up from that water.

This is true not just of poetry but of all the recording arts. Jerry Uelesman, a friend of mine who's taught photography for many years, often sends his class of thirty or so students out to photograph the same clump of grass. And when one of them protests, "But we'll all take the same picture," and one of them always does, Jerry tells him, "Don't worry, you won't." And he's right. They don't.

Here's another example, closer to our own situation. I've done some work with kids as a writer in the schools. One year, I decided to try a mock translation exercise with seventh graders. After they finished protesting, "But I don't speak French," and I finished telling them, "I know, that's why I'm giving this to you," they settled down to work. As the room quieted, I started worrying. I'd given them all the same poem to "translate," because it had obvious cognates, which I'd thought would lower their resistance to the process. What if they all came up with the same "translation?" When I saw the results of the exercise, I was immensely relieved to see that not one of my students had come up with anything that resembled the poem anyone else had written. Sure, they'd used a lot of the same words, but the emotional thrusts of their "translations" were completely different from each other. They didn't arrive at finished poems by doing this, any more than you will. But they did end up with a few good lines each, out of which they cobbled (with my help I admit; though I never added anything to what they wrote, I did, often, suggest subtractions) some pretty amazing work. No one I've ever shown that set of poems to has failed to be astounded that they were written by-twelve-year olds.

GOING FOR IT

So, here we are. Stop reading (for now) and get out there. Find a nice space. Get your own box of crayons. Enjoy yourself. You'll know you'll have it knocked, if, when you look up from your typing or writing, you're astonished at what time it is because you hadn't noticed the hours going by. That happens because at some point in the process, without seeing the guards or customs agents, if they were there at all, you'll have crossed over a border. You'll have been in a zone where there is no time, where all calls are free and you never know who's going to answer when you pick up the phone, which in that universe won't be ringing, but will be meowing or tweeting or bleating like a calf. Hear that *Baaaa?* It's for you.

EXERCISES
Going Fishing

Because getting started is the hardest thing to do for most of us, there are more exercises in this chapter than in any other. You'll notice that a few of them don't involve writing. What you're after right now is to develop the kind of prepared mind that chance will favor.

AT THE SUPERMARKET

1. Pick a lowish number before you go in. Go to the aisle that matches the number, and write down the items that are sold there. If the brand names interest you, write those down too. You should have a list of at least twenty words. At home, sit down and write a stream-of-consciousness "spill," using at least ten of the words on your list. Don't go for perfection, and be sure not to read what you're writing as you go along. If you do that, this little voice in your head will be saying, "Oh, that's not very good," and "Oh come on," and you'll get blocked.

2. Go to any aisle you choose. Really look at one thing in that aisle. Now, imagine how it would feel to *be* that thing, or, alternatively, what you would like it to tell you. Here's a poem of mine that began with this sort of expedition—in my case to the frozen food section.

Aquarium

Here behind glass they are stacked
in schools. Far from the leaping cold
of Iceland, cod wait without their hearts.
Here, headless shrimp crowd together.
Here are salmon, carved in flat lyres,
that we may know them by their color only.
And look, children, here are the smelts.
They have left them whole.
Do you think, if we take them home

and thaw them out, they will show us
what it was like to swim, thick as shoppers,
down the dark aisles of the sea?

IN THE CAR

1. Register every physical detail you can about the driver in a car stopped at a light next to you. Describe the car in your head too, including how it's kept up. Is it dusty? Is there a dent in the driver's side fender? When you get home, write down as much as you can remember. You can use this watching exercise several ways after that. Write about the car, thinking how it resembles what you imagine the driver is like—the way they say dogs look like their masters or long-married couples look like each other. Alternatively, describe the house you think the driver left just now. Talk about the place he/she is headed. The point of all this is that when you write poems, the detail in them won't always come from what's right in front of you. In fact, sometimes, like any painter, you'll find yourself having to invent it. If you aren't in the habit of sharp observation, you won't have any visual reserves from which to draw.

2. Use your driving time to work on memorization. Try to learn a poem a week. If you do this faithfully, you'll have subconsciously improved your musical ear and you'll have acquired a repertoire you can delve into whenever you like. You may think you can't memorize poetry. Can you sing songs? Of course you can. Well then, you can memorize poems.

AT HOME

1. When you're cleaning up, pick something you're using, like the dust rag, the mop, the broom, the vacuum cleaner.
    a. Think how you'd see that object if you were a Martian. Squint, like a kid looking at clouds. What does it look like? An animal? A plant? An old dress? What?
    b. What if that thing rebelled? What if all the cleaning equipment got together and went on strike? How would their manifesto read? What sort of government do you think they'd set up? What do you think your part in the new order might be?
    c. Trace the history of one of those objects in one of two ways: from its origin (tree to broom-handle, etc.), or by writing the story of its life once established as a broom/rag etc.

2. Go to a drawer in your kitchen (not the one with the knives). Reach in without looking and pull two things out. Go to your writing space and start typing. What's those objects' relationship to each other? What happened between them just now, when the drawer was closed?

3. List what you'd carry out of the house if there were a fire. Take the first five things on your list.

   a. Write an exact prose description of one of them without naming it. Don't use adjectives. Don't try to write a poem. If you were going to take a photo album, describe the album itself, not a photo.

   b. Describe the object again, but this time thinking of a person you know well. You're not allowed to name the person. If you have a good friend, someone who won't judge your writing (because you won't have a finished piece right now), show it to her and see if she can guess who you're talking about.

4. Describe the food on your dinner plate as a landscape.

5. Go to your bookcase and scan the titles. Write down a list of at least ten of them in an order that appeals to you. I owe this one to my singer-songwriter son. When he was in high school, he used to come up with amazing song lyrics. Finally, I asked him where he got them, and he said, "Look at my bookcase."

6. Describe something in your closet in terms of a relationship important to you. Don't overlook the hanging rod, the hangers themselves, shoe-trees, hooks, and so on. Here's a poem of mine that started like that.

The Shoes

> They were wine suede with just a thin strap
> across the ankle. Sometimes I could tell
> they were wrong, but I didn't care.
> I wore them with everything. When they began
>
> to sag, it was only a little at first, like shoulders
> at the end of the day, and it didn't matter that
> my feet slid extra with each step. I pulled the strap
> tighter. It bit a new hole. Then their color

turned sad and stains started to rise up their sides.
Water markings, the wavy outlines of tears. And
underneath how thin they grew, how easily
small stones would bruise. A heel came loose.

I nailed it back. But the nail head worked through
to my bare heel and every left step pained.
I took the shoes downtown. The aproned cobbler
turned one over, gave it back. These are too far gone,

he said. Buy yourself some new shoes, he said.
The sun hit the floor like new leather, hard and raw.

ANYWHERE:

1. Bring back an odor that has had real identity for you. Describe the place that odor takes you, specifically enough so that a blind person could "see" it. How old are you now? Write as fast as you can, from the point of view of your younger self. Start in the place with the odor, but don't try to legislate where you go from there. Think what every noun you use might be like, and, as often as you can, substitute the image for the thing. For instance, if the odor was the slightly sour odor coming from a culvert you used to crawl through, you might think that on end the culvert looked like a circle, or a wedding ring with a river at the bottom and you'd begin with that.

2. As you'll have already seen, I like the possibilities of shoes. Start being aware of what people you know well are wearing on their feet. Sooner or later a pair will strike you as being just like, say, old Ed. Describe it—type, color, general size, degree of wear, location of wear—as exactly as you can, using the adjectives you'd apply to Ed if you were writing about him. Don't forget to notice if the shoes are different from each other.

3. Cut a picture out of a magazine—Sunday supplements are good for this—and describe it as something else entirely. Don't think, just type. Or take another picture and type what happens next. There's a chair in the picture. Go on. For instance: "Its seat is still warm, as if an oven had been left on inside, the young wife with her burned arms sets down the cake she's baked, she thinks he will not like it after all." And so on.

CHAPTER

2

HOW TO REVISE

I've heard people say that once they've been inspired to write a poem, they don't want to change it. If you ask them why not, they often tell you that they think that editing the poem will inevitably do violence to their impulse in writing it. For years, I thought this idea was just plain wrong-headed. Until I heard a young man read, at a coffee-house open-mike session, a poem he'd written to a friend. I remember being touched by the boy's heartfulness, and I also remember being glad he wasn't my student because the poem itself was so clichéd. A few readers later, this young man came over to my table (I was the featured performer that night) and asked me how he could make it better. At first I didn't know quite what to do. But then I did: "Don't change a line," I said. "Your friend is going to love it." I think that was the right answer, because his poem was going to accomplish so perfectly what it came to do that it didn't matter that it wasn't poetry in the art sense of that word.

OF HEART-POETRY

Here's what I mean. When we heard the poem, it made all of us smile because it was so deeply felt, but once the boy stopped speaking, it wasn't going to exist, because there was nothing in its language personal to him. To change that, he'd have had to throw everything he'd written away and start over. And there was no real reason to do that, because the message of the poem was its real reason for being.

I think it's important—really important—to honor heart-poetry. But if that young man's true motivation had been equally poem and message, then my answer would have been completely different, because when you're talking about poems as art, very few are born perfect. Okay, once in awhile—but not often and never a very long poem. If someone tells me all his/her poems slide out in finished states, then I get immediately suspicious because the old saw about genius being one percent inspiration and 99 percent perspiration applies to poetry as much as it applies to anything else. And writing poetry that has a chance to last is work. It's wonderful, rewarding work, but still work.

WHY "EDITING" ISN'T A BIG ENOUGH WORD

So let's assume you're ready to work/revise, which presumably you are or you wouldn't still be here, right? Now what? Well, I'm about to tell you as much as I can, but before I do let me clear something up. Often, people call the process of getting from started poems to finished ones "editing." But in my experience that's not really accurate, because editing means taking what you have and cutting or rearranging it until you have something clear. When I work on poems, I do all that, but most of the time I end up adding something in the process, and more often than not, what I add is what turns out to make the poem work for me.

The bad news is that I can't tell you how to get to that "aha" adding moment. I'd love it if I could, because then I wouldn't have to go into every new-poem session feeling insecure. But the good news is that if you work hard enough, it's bound to happen for you, and when it does, you'll go around the rest of the day feeling as if you've just taken some mind-altering substance. You'll be floating. It's the best way to lose weight in the world.

BEGINNINGS

Ready? Let's get down to specifics. Though of course what happens all through any poem is important, beginnings and endings are crucial. Do you remember when you were a kid and someone bought you animal crackers in that box built like a circus wagon? What was the first thing you did? Take a cracker and bite off the heads and legs, right? Once you'd done that, a camel looked like a hippopotamus looked like a lion. In other words, heads and legs were how you told one animal from the others. Well, beginnings and endings are heads and legs. They're the poem looking at you, and the way the poem walks away, and together they make the poem a whole animal.

It's obvious that beginnings are important. Poems aren't novels or even short stories, because in a poem you don't have time to set the scene. You have to grab your reader now, or she's off down the street having coffee with someone else. This is especially true of magazine editors, who have stacks of submissions to get through and not much time to get through them. This doesn't mean you have to start your poems with an overt attention-getting device like a four letter word. But it does mean you need to get your atmosphere straight in a hurry.

Now when you were trying to generate raw material, where you started didn't matter. But once you reach the rough draft stage, it's different. Suppose you were telling me about your vacation. If you were doing this in stage one mode, you might start with how you dragged the suitcases out to the car. You had to drag them because they were so heavy you couldn't pick them up. Then you'd explain that after you loaded up the kids, you realized you'd done something odd with the keys. Then you'd tell me how you had to turn the house upside down until you finally located the keys in the bathtub, by which time the baby had thrown up on the four-year-old. So of course then you had to clean both of them up and settle them back down, and then, finally, you pulled out of the driveway. Then there was the long stretch on the interstate between home and the mountains, where you kept the older kids entertained by playing the let's-see-how-many-different-license-plates-we-can-spot game. At the end of all that explanation (and it was dark by then), you tell me how you pulled into the condo. Well, guess what? Your vacation really starts there. That was the story you came to tell.

What I mean by this is that most of the time I'm not sure what I'm getting at until I've gone through a lot of preliminaries, which were the equivalent of warming up the car for a trip. I tend to forget to cut the warm-ups when I start editing, I think because on some subconscious level they feel lucky since they were what got me here and in a pinch I superstition they could get me back, like the crumbs in the Hansel and Gretel story. Sometimes too, I don't realize how superfluous all those preliminaries are until I look at the whole thing one morning and it's suddenly clear that the twelfth line is where the gears kick in. So I cut the first eleven lines, and now the poem starts where it should have all along.

The point I'm trying to make is that you should always suspect the beginnings of your poems. Always ask yourself if the first few lines are the most vital place the poem could possibly have started. And in the process, keep in mind (I haven't mentioned this before) that what you thought was the beginning of the poem might have been, all along, the end, or vice versa. What I'm getting at here is that when you're thinking about beginnings, you should look everywhere and not stop looking until you're sure.

AND ENDINGS

One way to finish a poem is to tie the last couple of lines back to the first, like one of those stoles where the tail locks into the mouth of the skinny little thing with the beady eyes (which at this point in the thing's life really are beads). That's a time-honored approach and one we've all used. The only thing you need to be aware of is that that approach to closure can be addictive. I'm not knocking closed systems. Take a polished stone, for instance, to which surfaces nothing can be added. But if you use them all the time, your work gets predictable, otherwise known as "boring." Besides, sometimes the beauty of a last line is that it opens a poem wide. Poems like that are boxes left open so the world can fly in.

If you work your little fingers to the bone and every ending idea you come up with is either predictable or forcibly closed, try reverting to draft mode. Take the couple of lines that lead up to your end, and, starting with those, writing as fast as you can, fill a whole page. Sometimes when you look back at what you've written down, there it is: right in the middle.

HOW TO CLUSTER, FOR ENDINGS OR OTHERWISE

Another way to break the deadlock is to try my version of clustering. This can be really helpful not only with endings but also when you aren't sure where you are with a particular poem or when you know more or less what feeling you want but not specifically how to get at it.

I first came across clusters when my son was in middle school. One afternoon, I asked him what all that scribbling was, because he didn't look like he was doing homework, and he said, "It's for English, Mom. Miss Greenhalch is making us do a cluster with the assignment." He'd written his essay (on *The Grapes of Wrath*, as I remember), and now that he was finished, he was generating a cluster to turn in. It was supposed to have been the other way around. Clusters (a.k.a. mind maps) are supposed to unlock your creative juices, and you're meant to go from them to the finished product, not in the reverse direction. At the time, I thought clustering looked like a gimmick too. It reminded me of the "new math" my kids used to come home with, which gave them absolutely no clue as to what would happen if you had three apples and gave one away.

But after I'd thought about clusters a while, it occurred to me that if I approached them a little differently, they might be useful after all. So I tried doing a cluster for a poem I was stuck on ("To Play Pianissimo" in my book *Forty-Four Ambitions for the Piano*). It worked! Then I tried it again with another poem in that same book, "Octave." It worked again. That was beginner's luck. Clustering's no magic bullet. I will say, though, that it's helped me get past the predictable more than once. I think it works because when you cluster you're not under pressure; you're just making associations. You're not expected to, in fact you shouldn't, have a final product in mind. Of course, under your breath, you do, which is why coming up with a really good cluster sometimes finds you what you're looking for.

Here's generally what to do. Get a sheet of typing paper and write in the middle whatever feeling or idea you want to get at with the end of your poem. Let's say it's "loss." Draw an oval around it. Now ask yourself: what color is loss. Okay, blue, purple, black. Write those down, each one circled and connected to the center with a line. It will look a little like a daisy. Now, what else is black? Okay, "night." Draw a line out of "black" and write "night" at the end of it. Draw an oval around "night." What does night make you think of. Write "stars." What rhymes with "night"? Okay, "fight." Write it in. That is, a line and oval out of "night." What does fight make you think of? Write "mother." What rhymes with mother? Write "smother."

Now, back to loss. What sound does loss make? Write "whimper." Write "silence." Write "scream." What color is scream? Write "red." What sound does red make? Back to loss. How does loss physically feel? Write "smooth," write "stone," write "marker (grave)." Write "empty." What else is empty? Write "wastebasket." Where is a wastebasket? Write "bedroom." What did you last see in a bedroom? Write "mother." Write "stained sheets."

What does loss smell like? Write "musty." What else is musty? Write "a shut-up drawer." And so on. I've put the cluster I've been talking about on the following page here, so you can see what's happened so far. There aren't any rules, just go out from each word using questions from the five senses, rhymes, free associations, anything you can think

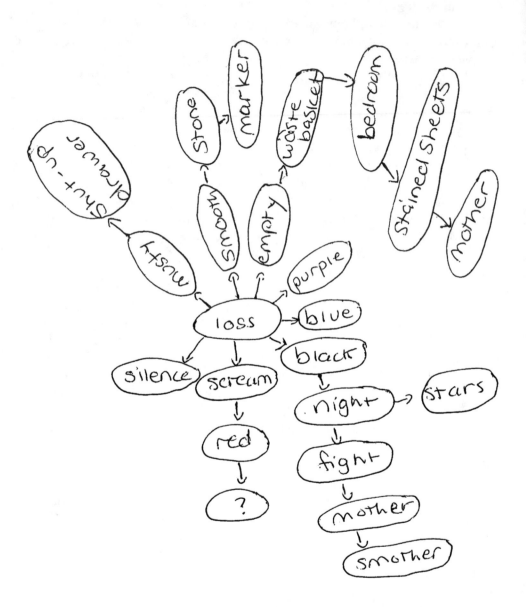

of. Don't read anything more than the word you're associating at the moment.

Once you've filled a page, look back at it, and try joining words from as far apart as possible in the cluster. Say "red mother," "musty night," and so on. See if one of those can trigger your last line.

The Importance of Giving Up Control

Before I leave the subject of endings, I want to tell you about a common mistake. It happens because we have good intentions. We want to make sure our reader doesn't miss out on what we've been trying to convey. So, to help her out, we sum it all up for her. Sometimes we do it with really flat lines. Sometimes we do it by overloading some image to the point of burnout. Sometimes we do it by providing a list of images, all basically conveying the same idea. Those approaches won't work because the reason you write a poem isn't to make some linear point. If you'd wanted to do that, you should have written an essay. You want instead to get at a feeling that often can't even be named with a single word, to get at something ineffable (I love that word!).

When you evoke that ineffable emotion, which you do by being very specific, you should trust your reader to get there for herself. Otherwise, she has the perfect right to get annoyed because you're clearly trying to push her around. It's like someone who tells you how to find a site you've been looking for on the Internet, then stands behind you watching every keystroke, bending over you to get his hands on the keyboard so he can do it for you. Doesn't that drive you crazy? Sure it docs. Besides, guess what? Once you've written this poem, it doesn't belong to you any more. It belongs to the person reading it.

From time to time, I've seen essays students have written about my own work. Seldom did those essays describe what I thought I was doing when I wrote the poem or book of poems. When they did, I was happy of course, but, on the other hand, I've been thrilled by what these people had seen in my poems that I hadn't. "Look at what was in there," I'm thinking, "and I didn't even know it! How great!" This kind of thing happens because poetry comes not out of the "let's-make-this-clear" part of the mind but out of the subconscious.

When I write, I've learned to trust my instinct to find the details I want, meaning that I've trained myself to stop thinking at the point at which those images *feel* right. So of course it often happens that there are implications to the details I've chosen that I didn't consciously intend but which are no less there because of that. In fact, I truly believe any poem at all can legitimately have many interpretations, because interpretation necessarily involves a reader, and a reader is always going to filter its imagery through his/her own life. The real wonder and beauty is that in spite of all our differences, we find such passionate, deep connections with each other through poems.

It's because I've both felt and witnessed those deep connections that I have issues with English teachers who tell their students that their interpretations are "wrong" when they don't happen to match what the critics think. I've met many people over the years who, not surprisingly, have been put off poetry for life because of the Cs and Ds they got on high-school English papers. Which is a huge pity in light of the fact that poetry's for everyone and readers have a perfect right to get out of a poem whatever walks over and bites them, and to hell with the parasitic critics.

If you agree with this, you're going to have to credit it as it applies to you as a writer. In other words, you're going to have to let your readers draw their own conclusions. If you've chosen the right details for your poems, then most readers will get out of them exactly what you intended. But if they don't, be glad. Look at all you did without even knowing it.

Let me say this one more time. Never end a poem in a way that backs your reader up against a wall with your metaphoric finger jabbing into his chest. Finish it without comment, and leave it at that. The longer you write, the more comfortable you're going to be with this idea, so if it makes you nervous now, do it anyway. Trust me. You'll feel differently after a while.

WHEN TO STOP WORKING ON YOUR POEM

Poems need, by the time you let them go, to be as close to perfect as you can make them. "But how do I know?" I can hear you asking. Well, the fact is that it does take experience with your own writing to be certain, and even then you can't always be. But here's a stab at how to tell you're through. You have your poem where you want it when: 1) you've started at the beginning; 2) you're in love with the way it ends; 3) adding a comma or taking a word out would change the meaning; and, 4) only you could have written this poem.

More about Number Three: The Usual Suspects

We've already covered beginnings and endings (a.k.a. one and two), but what's behind three and four needs some discussion. Fulfilling requirement number 3 nearly always involves pruning, since not-yet-edited poems tend to be weedy. Begin by cutting any words or turns that don't absolutely have to be there. This applies even when your poem's tone is conversational, because if you don't cut digressions, you'll find yourself piled up on them the way a canoe piles up on sunken logs.

Now as you squint around with your pruning shears, here are some things to squint for: clichés, abstractions, adjectives, and connectives.

Clichés

Read through the poem and see if any phrases sound at all familiar. If they do, they may be clichés or, worse, plagiarized. Google the suspects. If they're someone else's lines, either cut or acknowledge them. If they're clichés and you're especially fond of them, you can sometimes rescue yourself by turning them around. Country songs do it all the time—but don't you, or your poetry will get mannered and lose its edge.

Abstractions

It's risky to use abstractions, especially if you're a beginning writer. They don't taste of anything, smell like anything, make any particular noise. In other words, they don't in themselves say anything about you. When you catch a word like "love" or "fear" in one of your poems, go ahead and cut it, and if the idea was important to you, find something idiosyncratic—and physical—to put in its place. If you get stuck on this, try clustering. Put the abstraction into its little cage in the middle and fill the page. Your poem will be the more muscular for it and the reader is much more likely to care too, because now it's personal.

I don't mean to suggest by what I've just said that you should never under any circumstances use an abstraction in a poem. When you're starting out, I do think you shouldn't. But as you get more skilled, you'll learn to make abstractions work. But don't use them often, and when you do use them, be sure they're paid for. It takes a lot of details to buy one abstraction, and if you haven't earned it, you'll be sorry because it's going to fall flat at your feet, clunk.

Adjectives

Next to abstractions, the next most abused-by-beginners category of words would be adjectives. Adjectives are spices like coriander and garlic and ginger. It's true that they can make food interesting, but like coriander and garlic and ginger, they need to be used with discretion or they'll be all you taste. Here are some general principles. When you use an adjective, it should work like the kind of ending that opens up rather than encloses. Think of something that normally would be seen as completely *un*like the noun it precedes. Think of the noun in as new a context as you can, like the ocean or the sky folded into a drawer, and that may do it for you. Then, try to avoid adjectives that are implied in the noun they precede—like "little child." (Sure, sometimes it works—I remember "and a little child shall lead them" too, but it's rare). Then, try not to use any obvious ones, even ones that add to the noun. Suppose you wanted to describe a chair. If you said "overstuffed chair," that would do it, but this is a poem, and "overstuffed" is boring when it's used with "chair." You might think of this sort of adjective as an abstraction in drag and try to get more vivid. Imagine the chair as a person maybe, think of something else that's overstuffed maybe. It's your chair. In other words, when you use an adjective, it should either expand the universe within which the reader understands the thing you've named, or it should make the reader *see* the thing non-generically. Otherwise, leave it out.

One way to tell where you really want your adjectives is to cross every single one of those suckers out of your poem. Then retype/write the poem and read it again. See which of the deleted words you miss. Then take another, tough look. Are the adjectives you're tempted to repatriate implied in their nouns? Are they abstractions in disguise? In which case, replace them or leave them out entirely. If you decide they add to the freshness of the poem, no problem. Keep them and good for you!

If there are nouns that you decide on second or third reading do need adjectives, but the ones you have aren't it, cluster. But no matter what, when you're through with the poem, you shouldn't have many adjectives left. As I said a minute ago, adjectives are seasoning and you want to be judicious.

Connectives

Watch out for connectives. Words like "and," "next," and "then" tend to be redundant, because if one sentence follows another, you already have sequence. The exceptions are mostly related to tone. For instance, using "and" can create a story-telling voice. As you may have noticed reading this book, I'm personally a little fond of that voice. Still, in the abstract I do firmly believe in using connectives sparingly. So do what I say not what I do, as your mother may once, annoyingly, have told you—which made you go right out and do what she did, right? Which is why you may be drinking martinis with whole toothpicks full of olives even now.

Punctuation

Okay. When you're through with the words, go back and clean up your punctuation. This works on the same principle as cleaning up language: get rid of anything that can be implied. Commas at the ends of lines, for instance, are redundant because the white space there already implies a comma-length pause. If you want more than that, use a period—not a semi-colon because for my money, semi-colons against the right margin come off prissy.

Unless you want your poem to feel choppy, don't use a lot of punctuation in the middles of lines. If you want the pace there smooth but you also want lots of pauses, try adding an extra space or two instead.

Now some people use no punctuation at all, but that's tricky because poems without punctuation can look pretentious. Also, unpunctuated poems can be musically ambiguous, so if you decide to go that way, be sure your spacing clearly reflects the phrasing you want the reader to hear.

MORE ABOUT NUMBER FOUR: HOW DO YOU KNOW THIS IS YOUR POEM?

Now we come to my last point: being sure this is your poem. But before I start on that, let me say that this doesn't always apply, because not all poems you write will be intended to be your poem—and good on them.

People in every art form imitate. It's even important to do that—it's a way of apprenticing to the masters. My songwriter son, for instance, who started writing songs when he was about eleven, wrote in the styles of groups he admired until he was in his mid-twenties, and you'll often see art students in museums copying paintings because it's copying more experienced people that teaches young hands how to move.

When you *are* trying to write in your own voice, though, never leave off number 4. And be tough about it. If you started the poem with imitation but branched off from there, now is the time to cut back what got you going. Prune your poem/bush until every leaf is yours.

But pruning alone may not be enough to get you to your own voice. Look at the form of your poem to be sure the line lengths and verse structure you've used reflect the pace you wanted them to. See if you want to substitute specifics for any generic verbs (like "walk") in your poem. If your poetry persona is plain-spoken, you may not want to, but if it's not, you should consider it.

BEYOND LINE-EDITING

Everything I've said so far has had to do with micro-examination. Sometimes a poem needs global editing. We sometimes find that hard to see, because—and I learned this from programming—we're, usually subconsciously, so emotionally committed to our original approaches. I am, anyhow. Once I've decided where I think my poem is going wrong, I tend to keep trying to fix that section. And it takes me ages (notice the story-telling voice?) to realize that the problem is actually somewhere completely different from where I thought and/or often couched in lines I liked so I left them alone. Here's how I've learned to break that mindset.

Think about a long jump. The athlete stands back, readies him/herself, then takes a barreling run into the sand. When he reaches the takeoff point, he leaps. And, hopefully, lands at a mark that is a new personal best. Well, sometimes when I'm working on a poem that I think gets into delinquency somewhere in the middle, I do just what that athlete does. I start not at the leap, but at the run, by retyping my whole poem, starting from the first line.

When I do this, within two or three passes my fingers often find the problem for me. I think that's because typing from the beginning takes me back to why I was writing the poem in the first place, and going on from there can leap me over the rough spots. It's been on runs like this that I've most often come up with endings that sent me flying, not to mention seeing what, in the middle, deserved to be left in the sand.

ON TITLES

Let's assume you have your poem just the way you want it. Are you finished? Not quite. There's one more thing to think through, and that's the title.

Some people cop out of this whole issue by calling the poem "Untitled" or by using the first line as the title. That's okay I suppose, but they've missed an opportunity, because titles can expand the poems they go with. For instance, let's say you've called a poem "Leave-taking," but it's not ostensibly about that at all. So now the reader is going to think, "Hm-m-m, what's the connection?" and by doing it, get more invested than he/she would have been otherwise, and the poem too can deepen in the bargain. Titles that work that way are the ultimate gesture in the "show, don't tell" world.

No matter what, never slap something on top of your poem just because it looks bare without it. Titles like "Song," "Ode," "Sestina," and so forth are limp as old rags. To get at an interesting/useful title, try thinking of it as a line in the poem, only shorter.

Here's something else you might consider when the point of your first stanza or two is scene-setting. Try using your title to communicate that information. That way, you've freed your poem to begin in its real place. Or put a place/date/dedication tag line under an interesting title. One more possibility: using an epigraph as a tag line is a cheap way to add dimension to your poem.

Whatever you end up doing with your title, remember that anyone reading your poem is going to see it first and read on according to whatever it conveys. And if the title's boring...well, you get the idea. The point is that when you call your poem something, it needs to be for a reason that has to do with this poem and/or with yourself personally. You wouldn't have a baby and name him "Baby," would you? Well, maybe you would, but if you did, "Baby" wouldn't be so grateful when he grew up, and I'd look out, if I were you, when the kid reached his teens.

But seriously, folks, as they used to say in vaudeville (which even I don't remember, okay?), there's nothing I've told you about revision, including this last bit about the title, that you can't do. And when you get deeply into it, you'll find yourself in a double state, both far away from your life and, at the same time, closer than you could ever have imagined. Some day you'll brush one more coat of lacquer on that beautiful wooden egg you've spent weeks making, a coat no one will ever notice but you, and you'll understand in the deepest place in your heart that it was that last coat that made all the difference.

EXERCISES
Noticing Practice

PART ONE

Find a poem in a book of poems you like overall and see what you'd change if it were yours. Analyze what your principles were for the changes you'd suggest. Now go to your draft poems and find one where those principles apply.

PART TWO

Here are some segments of poems I've invented or adapted from lines I've seen in (good) magazines. See what you think. To save you flipping back and forth, here's what I've covered in this chapter: Beginnings and Endings; Extra words of any kind; Unnecessary Abstractions, Adjectives, and Connectives; Clichés; and Making the Title Work for the Poem.

If the segment begins or ends the poem, I've told you. Otherwise, consider it in the middle. My comments are at the end of the exercises, but *don't* look at them until you've worked through the segments for yourself.

1. He opened his huge, wide hands.
His wet eyes brimmed with tears.

2. (begins)
Elegy

Oh remember father, remember him.
How he would sit at his antique oak desk
built in the 1850s, composing his sermon,
hair snowy-white by then…

3. Not even Susan then, more like her mother that grew in a field, instead...

4. Trying to desire nothing, to be happy walking, I...

5. Already Melinda's words are changing. She is changing from lady to female to woman...

6. (END)

The light from her wedding ring shone terribly in her eyes.
She was sorry she married him.

MY COMMENTS:

1. "Huge" and "wide" aren't different enough to be interesting. Wide is better than huge. There might be a third word that would convey the idea—embodying what the hands are *like*, for instance. If his eyes brimmed with tears, they're wet by definition. Besides, brimming with tears is a cliché. If they brimmed with gin, *that* would be different. In other words, you can use a cliché if you give it a twist.
2. The title of this poem does absolutely nothing for it, especially because the first line sets the tone. Using titles like "Elegy," or "Song," or "Prayer" is pretty much the same as calling the poem "Untitled," which is simply the waste of an opportunity. Starting with "Oh" is tricky, but if you're skilled, it can work. But the first line is so vague as to be pretty much a loser. Father could be anyone, anywhere. You don't get to the action until you see him doing something. Now, OK, it's fine to say the desk is antique, but couldn't you describe it and get that across? And when it was built slows the poem down. The sermon addition is important because now you see father was a minister. "Snowy-white" doesn't cut it, because at least half of it is redundant. You could get it to a more interesting point by saying "his hair snow by then," which implies white without saying it.
3. Here's a grammar problem: Susan's mother "grew in a field"? Huh?
4. The second clause implies the first.
5. This is an interesting idea, but the start of the second sentence is clunky. You might be able to say "Already Melinda's word is changing, (because there's only one at a time and you want to emphasize the

naming), from "lady" to "female," etc.

6. The last line is an attempt to drive the point home which was well-made in the line before. Obviously, it should be cut.

CHAPTER
3
OTHER PEOPLE

JUST SHARING

Unless you're writing strictly for yourself, at some point you'll want to show your work to other people. It's important you tell the other person why you're doing that. If you want comments, say so, but if what you're really after is to share something you've written, then— especially if the person you're thinking of is close to you—be sure to make that clear.

When I was in my middle thirties, I started sending poems I thought were finished to my father. Each time I did that, Daddy would suggest radical changes. He'd been the editor of his college literary magazine, and he was trying to be useful. I understood his motivation, but his comments hurt my feelings anyway. And besides, his critiques weren't even helpful, because he came from a different era and our editorial eyes were completely different. These exchanges cast a shadow over our whole relationship until I finally realized that I should have made it clear I was only looking to share. Once I explained that, we both relaxed and everything was fine again.

But just saying you don't want comments may not be enough information. It may actually throw your reader into a panic. "If she doesn't want suggestions, then what does she want?" It can help a lot if you just say something like, "I just wanted you to see how much I cared about Aunt Mary," or, "This was a beautiful moment, so I wanted to share it with you," or, "I know I've looked down lately; maybe this will help you understand." Once she knows what you want, she can relax and enjoy your poems. Besides, setting all that up ahead of time is nice for you too, because it lets you sidestep the disappointment you may feel when what she comes up with wasn't what you wanted to hear at all.

Now it may happen that no matter what you do, you will find that someone close to you doesn't seem to understand. Maybe it's your wife or husband—let's say it's your husband who brings up every chance he gets that you're wasting your time, and that if you really want to write, you should try writing something that might sell. Or maybe the problem is that your husband is so used to reading for information that he finds it impossible—no matter how he tries—to understand what you're trying to do. After a while, you'll begin to notice even your most beautiful lines cringing when he looks at them. All of which may leave you feeling frustrated, even angry. But let me point something out that, if you believe me, will save you all this twisted energy.

Suppose you've been dating a mason. Suppose then that he takes you on a tour of the jobs he's proudest of. The house he slows down in front of, which to you looks exactly like every other house on its block, is an exceptionally fine pointing job to him. The side of the "Wal- Mart" which looks like just another Walmart to you, represents months of his tapping bricks into place so they're perfectly aligned with the string, all the while leaving behind so little mortar on the surfaces that the wall looks as if it might have been built by machine. Now be honest. No matter how you try to work up some enthusiasm, it's going to be clear to him that you don't get it. Think how he's feeling at the end of this, as the two of you pull into his driveway.

Or…suppose instead that you're a guy and your new love interest is a sailor, who spends all her time either working on her boat or thinking about it—how she can fabricate a part to fix the macerator or the winch that sticks, how she might trim the jinny next time so she can get an extra half-knot out of that following wind. You may think in principle that billowing sails and blue seas are poetic, but in practice what happens is that every time she starts in on one of her speeches, you keep smiling because you love her, but your inner face goes blank.

The point I've been trying to make, which I'm sure you get by now, is that the mason/sailor isn't going to change you and you aren't going to change the mason/sailor. The sub-point I'm trying to make is that that's okay. If you can stop wanting him/her to be more like you, maybe he/she will be more inclined to relax and let you be who you are. What you'll find after a while is that sharing your work with your partner-not-like-you will get easier, because you'll have stopped expecting from him/her what he/she can't give. And in turn he/she will be free to be proud of you, because you'll have stopped projecting the sort of discontent that naturally tended to stiffen him/her both against poetry and, by association, against you.

ONE-ON-ONE CRITIQUES

Once you've decided you're ready to go beyond sharing, you'll find that outside advice can be very helpful. Just be careful who you get it from. You might think someone who writes like you would be the best, but you may find that the comments of an open-minded someone who writes to a completely different drummer may be even more useful than your soul-mate's, because your soul-mate may share your prejudices. What I'm trying to say here is that the fit-the-feet-into-my-slippers part may be more important than the is-this-person-like-me part. One more thing to keep in mind—whoever she is…if the person you share with does nothing but praise, she may be a good friend, but she isn't going to help you get better.

I'm living proof of how helpful the right someone different from you can be. I have a friend, Sydney Wade, whose work is almost my opposite—her poems are lovely, quirky, and cerebral. But because she understands my shoes and I hers, we've been good for each other. She's showed me what language can do, and maybe I've showed her a little about emotional risk-taking.

Obviously, it doesn't always work that way. I've had it happen that the comments of people who don't write like me did me no good at all, because it was obvious that what they really wanted was for me to write like them. A case in point this way might have been Billy Collins who, when he was Poet Laureate, came to Ocala to read. In the Q & A afterwards, someone asked him how she could tell if a poem is good. He didn't hesitate a moment. "Well," he said, "You'll find that nearly all good poems begin x-way and end y-way" That's true of the way he writes, and he does it very well, but I couldn't help wondering at the time what effect he as a teacher would have on a younger me.

In the beginning, and maybe forever, you may find it helpful to pass your poems by a friend who reads but who isn't as sophisticated as you. You won't learn technique that way, but what you will learn is gold—whether what you've written will reach the general reader. Along those lines, my adult daughter, who reads a lot, but not poetry, has been hugely helpful to me.

Of course, if your poems are going to clarify and improve—and we all know that the only way to get better at tennis or any other sport is to challenge ourselves by playing against someone at least as good we are—at some point you'll need technical as well as general feedback. But again, don't be quick to jump. Consulting the most published person you can find may not be as useful as you'd imagine.

Before you expose your tender work, see if you think the person you have in mind can see from more than one point of view. If you think she can, before you ask her for comments, be sure to separate yourself emotionally from your poem, because if you can't do that, you'll find yourself defending your lines as if they were your children and nothing useful will reach you.

Now if it turns out that the person you've asked responds in such a way that tells you you were wrong about his/her openness, go ahead and write off his/her reaction. In a similar context, when I get turned down by magazines I'd like to be in (because they're famous) but whose editorial slant I don't actually like, of course there's a twinge, but the twinge comes with a message. It says "You idiot—what would it have meant if they'd taken this stuff—that you belong in a category of writing you don't care for in the first place?" So, in your case, if someone whose work you don't like doesn't like yours, so what?

LOCAL WRITING GROUPS

When you're ready to put your poems out beyond your immediate circle, try looking for a writing group in your community. Belonging to a group can shore you up if for no other reason than that for those few hours you'll be among people who understand why you do what you do. That in itself will be a relief if your work and/or family life is made up of people who think you're weird for putting a lot of time into anything creative that doesn't pay money. Second, attending a group that meets regularly puts a little healthy pressure on you to produce something. Otherwise it's easy not to write much, if at all. "Who's going to read this anyway," you'll be likely to tell yourself when the going gets tough, and you'll end up doing errands. Besides, if you're ever going to improve, you'll need the practice a group will stimulate. We all do. Need practice, that is.

To find groups in your area, look in the newspaper, check community bulletin boards, or ask at the public library. To find a good group, here are some things to keep in mind. First of all, you want one slanted towards poetry—at the very least, you want it to include several poets. That's because groups made up mostly of fiction writers tend not to be of much help to their poet members. You also want a group that's not the extension of its leader's ego (believe me, this happens). And you want one that includes at least a few experienced writers, so you can get advice on more than one level. If you think a given group might work for you, before you join, sit in on a meeting. If you aren't comfortable there, even if it looks good, try another one.

On-Line Groups

If for some reason a physical group isn't an option for you—you don't have time, there isn't anything locally, or you're shy but you still want feedback, look on-line. There are lots of websites (sponsored by magazines like *The Atlantic* or by private organizations like *Alsop Review*) on which you can post poems for comment. Lurk for a while to get an idea of whether the tone and level suit you before you jump in.

Actually, even if lurking's all you do, on-line poetry sites can be useful because the comments on other people's poems can help you think about your own. The downside to on-line, of course, is that there's no quality control. Still, I'm sure you'll figure out that when most of the comments resemble "Right on, sister," or "Keep that stuff coming," you're wasting your time.

If you do get involved with a web site, be aware that on-line life has the same potential pitfall for poets that café life had before it. It's seductive to hang around drinking wine and talking. But talking doesn't get art done. You have to be alone for that.

MFA Programs

If you get really serious about writing, you might at some point want to consider enrolling in a graduate writing program. There are two kinds of these: the traditional, two-year MFAs and the newer low-residency programs. Traditional programs are: 1) total-immersion, so you'd be living as a writer in an academic community of writers and, 2) generally oriented toward turning out "professional" writers. The thrusts of the low-residency programs vary. Some are as academic as traditional programs but others, Pacific Lutheran's, for instance, devote themselves exclusively to helping their students become writers.

You'll find the student bodies different in the two types of programs, too. Though the traditional ones can attract a mix of ages, the average is probably in the twenties. The low-residency ones, on the other hand—because they meet on campus only once or twice a year and the rest of the time work with a mentor by mail—draw a somewhat older group, the details of whose lives would have made a physical move impractical.

If you're thinking about either of these routes, here's the deal. Don't get an MFA because you want a job teaching writing. That isn't impossible, but it's also not likely, because there are many more graduates than jobs. And the jobs there are don't pay well, either, so unless you have a deep vocation for teaching, you're better off doing something else and writing in the time that's left.

If you do think you want to teach, here are some things to consider. While teaching feeds some peoples' writing, others find it drains them. It does drain me, because I use the same energy to teach poetry as I do to write it, so when I'm actively teaching, I can't work. When I taught Computer Science, I had no problem with that, because teaching CS drew from a different place: biceps versus triceps; riding a bike versus running.

Besides that, if you teach writing full-time, though you'll find some of your students' poetry stimulating, more often you'll find it completely unchallenging. and that can do you harm. For one thing, the Muzak-y drone of beginning poems may dull your ear. For another, it may tempt you to be satisfied with less than your own best work, just because anything you write is such an improvement on what you're getting from students.

If, after reading all this, you still think teaching writing would suit you, keep in mind that publication is as likely a way to get a teaching job as going the MFA route—that was how I got mine. I teach in a low-residency MFA program, which, as an aside, I find stimulating rather than the reverse, because the campus part of the program is so short and because I've always loved working one-on-one.

Okay—if what you want from an MFA isn't vocational but substantive, it's worth thinking about. But before you go one step farther, look in the mirror. Are you anxious to please? If so, is there any chance you might change the slant of your writing (and this would be subconscious) if you were sure that doing that would get you praise from your teacher or other students? If the answer to either of these questions is yes (and be honest), it isn't necessarily definitive if you don't know who you poetically are yet anyway. But if you're anyplace near what you think is your voice, and if you're at all insecure, I don't think a program is for you. It's too likely that you'd lose your spark, too likely that you'd migrate to the middle.

On the other hand, if one of the following describes you, then you may benefit from a program: You're a beginner, but you know who, independently of poetry, you are. Or, you're not a beginner and you're sure enough of your poetic identity that you can stand up for yourself when you think you're right *and* you're open to changing your mind when you think the other person is right.

If you fall in the above categories, then a good program, traditional or low-residency, can do a lot for you. First, it will give you a community of like-minded people—which is a wonderful feeling, because suddenly you don't need to explain. Second, if it's a good fit, it can move you toward your voice faster than you could have moved alone. But you do need to understand that no program can teach you to write. Only practice can do that, and a lot of reading.

Here's what to think about when looking at a program. First, consider the management. A select few programs are so toxic they should be designated as superfund sites. An acquaintance of mine, who got his MFA from one of those programs, told me that he'd been so devastated by the experience that he hasn't written anything since he left—and it had been three years. This sort of thing happens when teachers foment such a competitive atmosphere that instead of helping each other out, students spend their energies thinking about how they can shoot the competition out of the water. Or when they so overtly favor certain students that everyone else in the class ends up feeling invisible.

If the person in charge seems fine, then try to get a sense of the teaching styles of the faculty member(s) you'd be most likely to work with. Some well-meaning professors —and it's difficult not to do this— subconsciously guide their students towards their own styles. I've seen that a lot in art. My son's kindergarten class, for instance, turned out astonishing stuff. The only problem was that each kid's picture was a clone of every other kid's. On the other hand, gifted teachers, of art or anything else, can bring out the best in students as different from each other as chocolate and salt. Go to any school exhibit and look at the teacher's names on the students' pieces. You'll see what I mean.

Specifically, here's how to find yourself a good match. See if your favorite writers are teaching anywhere—but be clear that wonderful work doesn't necessarily translate into a gift for teaching. Then, check out some students who've been through those programs (any program will be glad to send you a list of its successful graduates). Ask them what kind of experience they had.

If you find yourself seriously interested in a traditional program, be sure to visit before you commit. Hang around the halls. Sit in on a workshop. How's the atmosphere? Does the instructor see the class as all about her? Would the kinds of comments she's making be useful to you? How about the feedback students are giving each other? Write down your questions to yourself before you come, so you can pay full attention while you're there. The bottom line, of course, is right-brained. Do you think you could be happy here? By happy, I don't mean do you think you'd get only positive comments. I mean do you think you could learn something.

On Criticism

Whether you join an MFA program or a group or get your comments on line, when you first start getting critical feedback, it's going to be hard not to take it personally. With time, if you've made a wise choice, you'll realize that what you and the other members of your group are trying to do is to make each others' poems clearer, leaner, more beautiful. Still, there will be times you find yourself thinking, "But I liked that. But that was my favorite part." When that happens, take a deep breath, mark the comment on the page, then go home and mull it over. At the end of the day, you don't have to agree with anyone's comments—the poem is yours and no one else's—but it's important to keep an open mind, even when you think your critic is wrong.

When I have negative reactions to comments—and of course sometimes I do—I think about what I know from my other life, which is this—when I have an error in a program, as its author I'm going to be the last one to see it. That's because though I think I'm open-minded, I'm usually subconsciously convinced that my code will work the way I thought it would. That's true of my poems, too, and it will be true of yours. Over and over, other people will pick out mistakes that in retrospect will look obvious even to you.

And speaking of finding mistakes—one spin-off of participating in a group may be that you'll discover you're terrific at diagnosing other people's problems. There's big satisfaction to that, more and more as time goes on. And no matter what, the more time you spend with other people's poems, the better you're going to get at your own. After a few years of this, you too may experience the sense of power a chef has when he's using a really sharp knife.

Here's the bottom line: when you show poems to other people, listen to what they tell you with as open a mind as you can. But, and this is important—in the end you should feel free to disregard their advice. Each person is his or her own animal, and if a giraffe tells you to do X, a zebra might well swear you should do Y instead. I do think, though, that if three people whose opinions you respect point to the same part of your poem and tell you there's a problem with it, then you should give that area serious consideration.

Of course, you can ignore your three people, four people, twenty people even, because as I've said (and I meant it), this is your work. On the other hand, you should understand that you are responsible for the well-being of this poem. You birthed it, and your job is to teach it as much as you can, then send it out into the world. So if something is hard for you but good for the child, do it anyway. Then, when her plane takes off from your local airport and disappears into the blue, you'll be able to let her go. You raised her, and it's her world now.

EXERCISES
Stepping Into Air

1. Choose a few poems you might share (as opposed to get comments on), and figure out for two different people, maybe one relative and one friend—exactly what you'll say as your basis for offering the one(s) you've chosen. Then, do it. Afterwards, evaluate what happened. If it didn't go well, try to figure out why.

2. Step into the baby pool by showing one poem to one person whose professional opinion you'd like to know. Monitor your reactions to the comments. If they don't bother you, if you feel excited now about the possibilities, you may be ready either to work with this person or find a group. If you do feel threatened, either this was the wrong person or you aren't ready. Figure out which.

3. Read your local newspaper to see what writing groups are going in your area. Note the contact information. Call at least one of them. If you don't like the feeling you get from that call, call another. When you feel ready, go to a meeting of the one that looks most likely for you. You want to take this one step at a time, so the first time you go, just listen; don't bring anything of your own. If this group doesn't work for you, try another.

4. Go to the Gazebo at *Alsop Review* and read the comments offered on the poems submitted. Find a poem you think you can be helpful on, and add your own two cents. Do this a few times. When you feel ready, submit a poem yourself.

5. Teach yourself a breathing/relaxation technique (there are any number: try Buddhist literature, for instance) and use it when you get a rejection or a comment that upsets you. That way, when you go home, you won't take it out on your spouse/partner/children/cat. This is worth doing no matter what, because you'll find whatever technique you learn useful in all kinds of contexts besides poetry—like turbulence when you're flying.

6. If you find yourself even vaguely interested in studying with someone else, search the web for online MFA programs. Research one of them as I suggested in the chapter. This doesn't mean you'll do it, just that you'll be more knowledgeable and, as the Earl of Stirling said, "Knowledge is power."

CHAPTER
4
GETTING INTO PRINT

You'd think that tips on how to write better would be what aspiring poets would want from us more seasoned ones. But in my experience, what's much more likely to come up is requests for tips on how to get published. Their sources run the gamut, from programming students who bring their poems to my office hours, to people I meet at parties, to proud mothers I've never met. I get e-mails like this all the time: "My daughter's English teacher says her poems are really good, so I wondered if you could tell me where she can get them published?" Sometimes it's someone who comes up after one of my readings. Once, it was a couple—they'd met when she answered his ad for a wife. She was living in Texas at the time, and he was in Arkansas, but he said that as soon as he saw her measurements he knew she was the woman for him, so he hopped in his pickup and drove south to pick her up. They'd brought me a huge binder of her poems about the Trail of Tears, and wanted me to tell them which of the New York publishers would be the best. At that same event, and with the same mission, was a bus driver, who for years had been writing poetry while he waited between routes. I was happy for these people, good for them for writing poetry with such energy—and I loved meeting them. But in those cases, and in my experience, this is often true of people whose primary question is "How do I get published?" their question isn't as simple as they thought it was.

WHY YOU MAY WANT TO SELF-PUBLISH

Ask yourself what you're really after. Is what you want the most in all the world to see what you've written in print? If that's it, then you may want to consider publishing your work yourself. There's nothing wrong with that. Lots of fine writers—Walt Whitman, for instance—

have done it. If you go that route, then you won't have to deal with all the rejection that goes along with submitting your poetry to the big impersonal literary world, and, truth in advertising, the rejection never stops. Recently, for instance, the same editor who chose, and praised, my eighth collection unambiguously turned down my ninth. And this isn't rare.

If you did decide you wanted to do your book yourself, how would you go about it? Well, if you're comfortable with technology, you probably already know that there are some terrific desktop publishing programs. But, though it may come as a surprise to the younger generation, not all of us were using the Internet by the time we were three. If the whole thought of computers makes you break out, look in your yellow pages under "printers." Visit the ones whose ads look likely and ask to see samples of their work. Alternatively, you can send your manuscript away to a larger printer whose main business is books. Bookmasters in Michigan or Rose Printing in Florida, for instance, are excellent, reputable places. Keep in mind that if you do go with a printer, you can do it for a per-copy rate, which drops depending on how many books you order and is often as low as $2.00 a copy for, say 1000 copies of a 60-page book.

Thinking you want your book to get around, you may be tempted instead of doing any of the above to go with one of the New York publishers, which advertise they're looking for new authors. Generally, this is a bad idea. You may get a good product, but you'll pay much more per copy than you would if you'd just gone to a printer. And be warned: subsidy publishers' promises of getting the word out on you and your work won't have any practical effect, because even if they do advertise them (I've seen those ads in the *New York Times,* too), bookstores will take those presses' books only on consignment if at all, and reputable reviewers will ignore them. If you want distribution and any chance at a review, publish the book yourself, using an invented press name.

I brought out second editions of two of my books, because the presses that had published them (one trade publisher, one university press) weren't willing to reprint when the first editions were gone. I did that under the name "Betony Press," and it's worked fine for me. I've had orders for those books from Barnes & Noble, from Borders, and from Amazon. But orders like that have been sporadic, because without sales reps, real distribution is pretty much impossible and I, probably like you, can't afford to hire any.

Here's the bottom line. Self-publishing is a good choice if your main audience will be friends and family. It's probably not the best way to go if you want to be widely known as a poet or if your main goal is to sell books, because, realistically, only the exceptional self-published book, like *Leaves of Grass*, makes it into the big time. Still, it can happen, and probably, given the leveling effect of the Internet, it's going to happen more and more often as time goes on. And if so, why shouldn't it be you?

ABOUT PUBLISHING "COMMERCIALLY"

If what you meant when you asked me how to get your work published was how you can get it out in the literary world, then you're going to have to start with magazines because, I don't know of any book publisher that would seriously consider a completely unpublished manuscript. Be ready, because when you do submit to magazines, you're going to be going up against other people's standards, and the course of your pursuit, no matter how good you are, isn't going to be smooth. Still, there are all sorts out there, so almost no matter how you write, if you persist, it's likely there's at least one magazine that would be glad to include you, and equally likely that its readers would be glad to read you. Let's say though, just for the sake of argument, that you're aspiring to the big guns, magazines that you know get a lot of submissions. In that case, be as sure as you can be that you're ready for that. What I mean by "ready" is that you have not just one or two poems you're happy with but some accumulation of hard-worked stuff that you're pretty sure is in your own voice. If you look at yourself and find you're at that point, go for it.

My ex-husband had the shoot-high idea from the beginning. When he was in middle school, he wrote a saga about a Civil War soldier titled "To a Soldier, Dying Young," and sent it to the *Atlantic*, which rejected it. Not daunted, he then submitted it to *The New Yorker*, which also rejected it. He just couldn't understand what happened. Finally, I think, he decided that they must not have read it. I also think this stunted his whole career as a poet, because, telling himself they just weren't deserving of such genius, he hasn't sent anything to either of those magazines since. This is a sweet story, at least to me, but there's a serious point behind it. When I was talking about magazines that get a lot of submissions a minute ago, I didn't mean for you to start right in with the *Atlantic* and *The New Yorker*. I began somewhere in the middle, and so should you. How high in the middle depends on where you think you are with your writing when you're ready to share it.

HOW TO FIND MAGAZINES THAT MATCH YOUR STYLE

Once you've decided to try to place your poems in magazines, buy yourself a copy of the *Directory of Poetry Publishers* from Dustbooks, or *Poet's Market* (*Writer's Market* is OK, but *Poet's Market* is better, because everything in it will be relevant) from *Writer's Digest*. Sit down and go through it—this will take a long time—and highlight your possible targets.

How do you know which those are? Well, you can pick out the magazines that publish poets whose work you like (if you aren't reading poetry, the odds are you aren't ready to send yet). Or the magazines that happen to be local to you. Or the magazines whose editors you've heard of. Alternatively, you can check the acknowledgments page in a book by a poet whose work you admire.

Starting this way will get you a preliminary list of magazines. But don't, unless you already know them, submit anything yet. First read at least one issue of each place you think you might send to. In the process, you may find some poems you love or some new poets you'll want to see more of. But no matter what, familiarity with a magazine will help you make smart decisions as to which of your own poems its editors might like.

Now, it's obviously impractical to buy a copy of every magazine on your list, partly because that would get expensive fast and partly because unless you live in a big city, you won't find many of them—if any—in your local bookstore. But you can find most of them for free on the Internet (though not all, and not necessarily usefully, because even now some magazines aren't online, and others make you pay to read more than one or two poems). As you surf, you may come across other magazines that weren't listed in *Poet's Market,* either because they're too new or because they're strictly e-zines and print isn't how they generate submissions. When you do find a magazine on your list, you may also find its editors' taste isn't yours. That certainly happens to me, and when I know that, I try to resist sending anything to that place no matter how famous it is because I can be pretty sure I'm going to be wasting my breath (a.k.a. postage).

By the way, if you don't have a computer, don't despair. Just go to your local library, since almost all libraries these days have Web access.

While you're there, especially if it's a large or a university library, check out the current periodicals shelves, because sometimes just holding a magazine in your hand can tell you a lot about it. Besides, you can also, if you like it, go and browse back issues, too.

You've probably gathered from this that it matters which of your poems you send where. It does. I write in more than one style, and I know perfectly well that if I submit some of my more *outré* poems to, say, *Southern Review,* I'll be wasting my time. So I send them to *Five AM* instead, or to *Exquisite Corpse.* In other words, I tailor what I send—and so should you—to what I think the editors of a given magazine might be interested in.

WHICH POEMS?

Beyond that, how do you decide which poems to send out in the first place? Of course, the answer is your best, but how do you know which those are? Well, in the last analysis, of course, you can't know, but one criterion you might use is to ask yourself, toughly, if there's any chance that this poem sounds like whoever you've been reading lately—because if your work's derivative, even if it's well done, a good editor will spot you immediately—"That lilac perfume, I'd know it anywhere!"—and say "No" anyway.

Here's the heart of what to consider as you choose which of your poems to send away: choose the ones no one but you could have written. In contests I've judged, those poems jump out at me, because, even if they're a little rough-edged, there's clearly someone home behind them. And that person behind the door makes them stand out from the beautiful nothings. So, if you send out the poems that you're technically happy with that also expose the most of your particular life, you'll be on the right track.

MATCHMAKING: BE PERSISTENT

Once you have your candidates assembled, remember what I said: be careful with your choice of magazines. Think of yourself as a matchmaker. The sulky boy with the inward girl, the salesman with the girl who loves to give parties. And so on. But, and here's a reality check: just because you like some magazine, it doesn't follow that they'll like you. Or at least, maybe not for a while. Most good journals get backbreaking numbers of submissions, and the competition is heavy. Sometimes too, magazines have to get used to you, so you need to send a few times before they know you're serious. Or sometimes the particular poems you've sent didn't click. Don't despair. Maybe something else will. Pay attention to editorship. Some magazines rotate that. If it's one of those and it's been consistently rejecting you, hold out and don't send again until the editorship changes.

In the real world, submitting your work means sticking your neck out, and since it's often, even usually, going to get chopped off, you'll have to keep growing new heads. In other words, you're going to have to get used to being told (if you take it that way, which you shouldn't), that you aren't good enough. That doesn't stop just because you've published a book or two, but it probably hits hardest at the beginning, especially if you see your first round of submissions as a test. "If I don't get something taken within six months," you tell yourself, "I must not be any good." When you've been at this longer, you'll realize that whether what you've written is good doesn't depend on other people; it's your decision. Still, rejection's never easy. It's ironic, isn't it, that people who write poetry, who of course must be sensitive people on some level or they wouldn't be writing, are also firmly in the camp of people whose path inevitably includes a lot of disappointment.

Here are a couple of things to think about. First, the truth is that choosing among good poems comes down to taste. So if you've written well, there is probably someone out there who will like what you're doing. Second, it's a mistake to keep the wrong kind of score when you send your poems out. When you do finally get something accepted, it's not 216 (rejections) to 1 (acceptance). It's 1 to zero. It's like a soccer game. When the match is over, no one asks how many shots on goal it took you to come up with the final score. The only thing that matters is that, in the end, you scored a goal.

SOME SUBMISSION STRATEGIES

When you send poems to magazines, there are certain things you can do to maximize your chances of being taken seriously. When I was an editor—first of *The Devil's Millhopper* and later of *The North Florida Poetry Review*, it was obvious to me which submissions came from people who knew what they were doing and which didn't. So, in that spirit, here's how to put your best foot forward.

How Many Poems?

Never send just one poem, because a one-poem submission, unless it's to an anthology wanting poems about a certain subject, makes it look as if this is the only one you've ever written. And, obviously, if an editor thinks that, he/she is going to be immediately less interested in you. Besides, no one but a beginner would send just one poem, so it's a dead giveaway on the face of it. Three poems is a good number; two, if one of them is long or is a sequence made up of shorter poems. On the other hand, don't send a whole sheaf of stuff. We used to get ten or fifteen poems at a time from one rather well-known poet. It made us think that she hadn't cared enough about us to bother selecting something to send, so she just sent us everything. This was compounded by the fact that most of the pages of her submission had obviously been folded more than once. Sometimes, they even had coffee stains. Though she wasn't a bad poet, her whole approach made us tired. And when we were tired, we were reading with less interest than we'd otherwise have had. Another way to put this is that it's usually best to send only what will go under one stamp, which is three sheets and your return envelope.

Now…when you put your submission together, follow the basic courtesies. Make sure your poems are cleanly typed and readable (no old print cartridges!), and put your name and address on every page. Fold your poems together, not separately. Remember the poet I just told you about and never send anything that has stains on it (your tear stains over the last rejection, someone may cynically assume—or the coffee you spilled at your writing group) or has obviously been folded before. We editors like to think we're your first, not your last, choice.

Cover Letters

Cover letters are often used to introduce yourself as a writer, so, from that point of view, if you don't have a track record, you may decide not to include one. Even though it may earn you courtesy points if you thank the editors for reading your work, it's rare that the fact that your submission includes only poems and an SASE (self-addressed, stamped envelope) will prejudice anyone against you. If you do send a cover letter, any kind, keep it short. Don't tell the editor your life history. Don't explain the punch lines of the poems you're submitting. Don't list every group or teacher who's ever liked your work. Especially, don't list thirty-three publications in magazines no one has ever heard of. Do, though, say something specific about yourself, such as "My work has appeared in *Carolina Quarterly* and is forthcoming in *The Atlanta Review*."

If you can, also mention something you liked in the magazine you're sending to. But don't bluff. A couple of years ago, when I guest-edited a magazine, a submission arrived from a poet who said that while she couldn't claim to have been a regular reader of my magazine, she'd looked at several back issues and to her surprise found some excellent poems there. I was surprised, too, since the issue I was responsible for was the very first for this magazine and there were no back issues.

My own cover letters begin with something like, "Here are poems." I used to say, "Enclosed are poems for your consideration," but after a few years, that felt wordy. You may be more comfortable approaching things formally, though, in which case, be my guest. If the poems belong to a longer sequence or to a particular manuscript, you can mention that now. After the "Here are poems" sentence, I used to list my books and maybe a couple of my best magazines—like *The Atlantic* or *The Christian Science Monitor*. Now, I just mention the title and publisher of my most recent book. Then I thank the editor for his/her time. Thanking the editor is important to me, because I really do appreciate that he or she is going at least to look at what I'm sending, and besides, I know from having been an editor myself how much energy it takes to read all the submissions that appear in the mailbox. Finally, I sign the whole thing "Sincerely," write my name at the end, and tuck the letter inside the poems.

A good job on the cover letter may get you through the first screening, but it won't always matter. I've had my stuff come back with my carefully composed cover letter still folded in, which gave me the idea that no one ever did look at anything I sent. And that may have been true. Some magazines use screeners who aren't careful and others just aren't good with unsolicited submissions, period. *The New Yorker* in particular is notorious for losing them. Now they seem to be losing them in cyberspace, but not much else has changed, so don't take it personally if you send something to *The New Yorker* and in return get the silent treatment, as if you've offended your lover and he/she isn't speaking to you.

An SASE

The one other thing you need to be sure to do when sending to any magazine is to include your appropriately postaged return envelope (a.k.a. SASE). If you don't, you'll never get your work back, and it will be your own fault. I think a legal-size SASE is best. The 8-and-a-half by 11 ones make you look as if you think your work is too important to be folded, which in turn makes you look silly, and the smaller envelopes makes it look as if you think your poem is a love letter. Not a good idea.

One more thing: never send anything illustrated or otherwise embellished. I judged a contest once in which one of the entrants had cross-stitched her poems onto what looked like chair covers. I thought it was sweet, but I admit it made me take her work less seriously than I might have, and some people, seeing that violet and green thread, wouldn't even have read her entry.

HOW TO HANDLE REJECTION

When you do start sending your poems out and getting them back, you'll get an instinct just by picking the envelope up as to what it contains. For instance, if what I get back is thinner than what I sent, it probably means they've kept something. Thicker can mean that too, because it usually means there are permission forms inside. On the other hand, thicker might just mean the magazine's sending subscription forms with your rejection, which is cheap for them but probably not very productive, because what are the odds that you'll send them money when they've just told you you're a loser?

In any case, no matter what I say or what you tell yourself, you're going to feel a little down when you open that envelope and find your children inside, sent home from school with a printed slip. That's only natural. After all, you're human. The only problem is that unless you live with another artist, your significant other, however wonderful that person is, sooner or later is likely to lose patience with the fact that you're poor company tonight because three rejections came in the mail you picked up on the way home from work. I used to let bad news in the mail bother me to the point where I'd ruin perfectly good evenings every time I got any, which in those days was even more often than not. In fact, after a while, when I was feeling low for any reason, my husband would ask me, "What's the matter, did you get a rejection?" This annoyed me a lot, especially because it was sometimes true. So. If you do go public with your writing, your parent/lover/spouse is going to have to put up with you. If they occasionally get obnoxious about it, be nice. I know it's hard, but try.

Here's some motherly/sisterly advice. Don't feel guilty that being rejected affects you. It's just a byproduct of being sensitive, and it's good you're sensitive. On the other hand, don't be unrealistic and expect that your non-artist friends and lovers are going to understand exactly how you feel, because, really, trying to legislate that won't work, and, anyway, it isn't being fair to them.

Here's how I suggest you handle turndowns so they have minimal impact on you and on the people you care about: don't reject that surge of disappointment, maybe even anger, out of hand; just listen to it and when it's said what it came to say, let it go. Those feelings are part of the territory, just like mesas are part of the Arizona desert. Besides, it's a good territory, all things considered. You're becoming a part of a community bigger than yourself by sending your work out into the world. And keep in mind that the best way to put disappointment to bed is to turn around and send whatever it is right back out. Sooner or later, if your poems are good, someone will take them.

But, be realistic. If you're sending only to the top magazines and getting only straight rejections back (no notes from the editor), don't let it go on forever. Try looking through directories, in libraries, etc., for magazines that you like, but which aren't so famous. Start there and work up. This can prevent you from getting so discouraged you stop submitting altogether. After all, keeping yourself going is a legitimate and important part of the breaking-into-print business.

TRACKING YOUR POEMS

There's one further issue about publishing in magazines that I haven't yet mentioned, and it's one that inevitably comes up once you start sending out a lot. It's mechanics: how do you keep track of all those poems that are currently flitting around the country? And there's a secondary question—what do you do if, in spite of your world-class record-keeping, you end up in the position of two magazines taking the same poem?

Let's start with the first. When I started writing, back in the '70s, I kept an alphabetized index card file, one card for each poem in current circulation. When I submitted a given poem somewhere, I'd write the magazine down on that poem's card. Then, when the work came back, I'd cross the name off, but not so I couldn't read it, and if the poem had gotten any positive comment, along with the rejection, I'd star the magazine on the list. When the poem got accepted, I'd transfer its card to another file box, with the magazine that had accepted it circled. That approach, though, wasn't enough, because when I was putting a submission together for, say, *The Southern Review*, it would have been helpful to know which, if any, of my poems they'd liked before. and I didn't have that information in one place, because I was keeping records only by poem.

So I refined my system by keeping two sets of index cards: one by magazine, one by poem. If you have a computer, you can buy software written especially to track submissions (there are ads in every issue of *Poets & Writers*), but you don't need to do that. If you have Microsoft Office, you can use Excel, which is what I do. I put poem titles down the side and magazines across the top. When I send something out, I enter the date. When I get the submission back, I replace the date with an "N" for rejection or an "N*," if the magazine liked the poem but didn't take it. When a poem gets accepted, I delete it from the submission file and add it to another file in a Word document, in which I keep a list of accepted poems. Then, when I'm putting a book manuscript together, I can go through that list and make sure all the acknowledgments are correct.

ON DUPLICATE ACCEPTANCES

The above may sound organized to you, and I suppose in theory it is, but the fact is that in my family I'm known as "detail woman," because of my notorious inattention to detail, which personality defect means that every once in a while I send poems out in a hurry, or not from home, and don't write them down. Or I write them down in the wrong columns. The result of that has been that a few times over the years, I've had the same poem taken twice, and I've had to call the editors of one of the magazines and apologize profusely about withdrawing my submission.

A couple of times those situations happened because the second accepting magazine had had the poem so long I'd given up on it and resubmitted it elsewhere, but the others were just my fault. Sometimes, in cases of double acceptance, an ethical question will arise because the second magazine is more prestigious than the first. It's tough, but I really think you need to do the honest thing, which is to give the poem to the first magazine.

What about Simultaneous Submissions?

Another issue that comes up when you're submitting poems to magazines is whether you really have to wait that nine-and-a-half months while your target is theoretically thinking about it. Maybe you can send the poem someplace else while you're waiting. Is that ethical? Yes, if both magazines allow that. Look them up online or in your directory (go to a library if you don't have one at home). If both places don't specify that simultaneous submissions are okay, don't do it. I know it makes you wait longer to get a poem into print, especially since some magazines take so long to make up their minds, but the hard truth is that if you do submit simultaneously to magazines that frown on simultaneous submissions, sooner or later it's going to catch up with you, and editors aren't going to look positively on whatever you send them after that, whether the poems are good or not. Think about it from the editor's point of view. Why should he/she put all that time and energy into reading your work, when someone else may already have taken it. And that's a fair argument.

On the other hand, if a magazine does take unconscionably long to get back to you (over four months unless they've specified otherwise), you have an absolute right to query them. Write to the editor, enclosing a self-addressed postcard. Say in your letter that if you don't hear anything by some specific date—give them ten days from the date you think they'll get your letter—that you'll submit your work elsewhere. Then you're covered, and you can send your poems out again with a clear conscience. Courtesy between writer and editor works both ways. They owe you a fair shake. You owe them not to waste their time.

How to Submit a Chapbook/ Book Manuscript

So far we've been talking about publishing your work in magazines. But at some point you may want more than that. Let's assume you've published a lot of work in magazines, and you've assembled a chapbook or maybe even a whole book-length manuscript of your poems (see chapter 5 for how to do that). How do you go about publishing it?

It's harder to find a press for your chapbook or book than it is to find a magazine that will publish you. I have friends who are very good poets who have been looking for years. But that doesn't mean you can't do it. Of course you can. Start looking for a publisher the same way you began looking for magazines. You can look at books by poets you admire and see who published them or the chapbooks, which the poets will often have published first. Besides that, *Poet's Market* and *The Directory of Poetry Publishers* list a number of presses, who they've published, and what their reading periods are.

If you don't mind paying entry fees (and they can get expensive), you can try the contests. At least in that case you'll know that someone looked at your manuscript (which I can promise won't happen if you send it cold to New York City). There are, too, lots of contests whose prizes (which always include publication, and sometimes some money as well) are reserved for chapbooks or first book manuscripts.

By the way, don't think that the fact that a publisher charges a reading fee necessarily makes the press illegitimate. Some publishers raise their publication/prize money this way. Others, quite frankly, do it to keep submissions down to those who are serious, and to a number they, the publishers, can handle given their staffing constraints. You may be surprised to hear this, but it's true: several of the most famous literary houses in the country, presses whose names you'll know, have only two or three full-time employees.

Many chapbook/book contests are listed in *Poet's Market.* You can find out about others by subscribing to *Poets & Writers,* which comes out bimonthly. You'll find articles related to writing and writers there, as well as magazines advertising for submissions. If you're a beginner, it's a good idea to subscribe anyway, because *P & W* is a very useful publication and well worth reading if you want to keep up with what's happening in the literary world.

Contests aside, there are lots of presses that publish poetry, and your source of information for that will be, again, as for most information in this area, *Poet's Market.* You'll find that poetry publishers break down into three general categories—New York houses, university presses, and small presses. The first category is, unless you have contacts, usually closed to beginners. On the other hand, many university presses, and some small presses too, have open reading periods every year. But don't send your ms. out indiscriminately to every press with a reading period. Check the catalogues of publishers you're considering. See how many titles they put out per year. Look at who else they've published if you don't already know. By doing that kind of homework, you can usually get some idea of whether it would be worthwhile to send your manuscript to any given place.

Now, the same thing applies to books that applied to poems. If you really want to get your collection into print, you can't afford to be put off by rejection, even lots of it. Choosing one or two from a pool of publishable manuscripts is, again, obviously, a matter of taste. And strange things can happen along the way. A book of mine called *Hunger* won the Iowa Poetry Prize in 1992. After the contest was over, one of the judges, none of whom I'd met before, told me that each of the members of the committee had settled on my manuscript before they came to the final meeting. Here's the strange thing: I'd sent the identical manuscript to that contest for the previous two years, and although it had done well in other competitions, it had never even made the finals at Iowa. In fact, by the time the Iowa people contacted me, I'd forgotten that I'd entered at all and was getting ready to send the manuscript out again. So, you never know. And of course also you'll have heard the (true) stories about the number of times very famous books were turned down flat before they finally found homes. The bottom line is this: You know your work is good. Just keep at it, and sooner or later something will break. The difference between you and someone who doesn't succeed is going to be that they gave up and you didn't.

A FOOTNOTE ABOUT AGENTS

The good news is that when you have a relationship with a literary agent, that person takes care of the entire submission process for you. Not only that, but he/she has a better chance than you do of placing your book, because an important part of any agent's job is to develop contacts in the publishing industry. The bad news is that, though I know someone who handled poets when she used to be an agent, very few, if any, poets have agents. The reason for that is simple economics. The better literary houses— excluding the largest New York presses, which may do a few more—put out poetry books in editions of maybe 2,000 copies. Obviously, sales potential like that won't pay an agent's rent. It's uneconomic for them to represent poets, so mostly they don't.

Lots of otherwise intelligent people don't know this. My father, for instance, was always trying to set me up with people he knew who could "help me in the publishing business." Once, that meant an agent. This man listened very nicely to my brief-as-possible explanation of what I do, with Daddy on the other side of the table certain that his friend was going to sign me up any minute, and that this encounter would lead to publication for sure, and perhaps in the end even to a Pulitzer. Then Daddy's friend explained what I've just finished telling you, and our encounter was over.

While we're on the subject of Pulitzers, here's my personal Pulitzer story. Years ago, I got a letter from my grandmother congratulating me on my nomination. Since this was before I'd published a book, I was puzzled at first. Then I realized that my mother, ever desperate to have a respectable person for a daughter, must have written her mother that I was doing so well I'd just received this nomination. So I wrote my grandmother back that, well, there are lots of nominations this year, so that while of course I hoped to win, she shouldn't expect to see my name in the paper any time soon. She was satisfied with my answer, I think, and I'm sorry to say that both she and my mother died without ever having that particular hope fulfilled. I don't expect it to be fulfilled any time soon, and probably never. Which doesn't bother me, because prizes aren't why I write and not, I hope, why you do.

EXERCISES
What's Out There?

The purpose of these exercises is to familiarize you with places you might want to investigate.

1. At the library : Write down the call numbers for the following poets:

Tu Fu
Sappho
William Butler Yeats
John Berryman
Dylan Thomas
Sylvia Plath
Adrienne Rich
Lucille Clifton
Tess Gallagher
Jared Carter
Billy Collins
Ted Kooser

Go to the stacks and browse the shelves in the areas of those call numbers. Write down the publishers of any books that strike a chord with you. Check three out, and read them at home.

2. On the computer:

Type "poetry" into Google. You'll be amazed. Once you've done that, other than the idiosyncracy of what you may come up with, here are some sites which are worth spending time on.

Self-publishing (print on demand) sites:

a. Ex Libris
b. Publish America

General sites:

a. www.poems.com

 "*Poetry Daily*". This site has a new poem every day and spotlights magazines and book publishers. NOT poetry.com; that is a vanity site.

b. www.pw.org

 The site for "*Poets & Writers*." This site is a clearinghouse for information about writers and writing. It includes the magazine whose classifieds list contests, awards, magazines looking for submissions etc.

c. www.alsopreview.com

 "*The Alsop Review*." Not a magazine but a permanent showcase of writers. By reading around, you can see which you like and where they publish.

c. www.fishousepoems.org

An extensive archive of younger poets, most with books. Has audio of the poets reading their work as well as texts of poems and interviews.

Print Magazine Sites (high-level, both print and web magazines):

a. *Georgia Review*
b. *Southern Review*
c. *Prairie Schooner*
d. *Beloit Poetry Journal*
e. *The Atlantic*
f. *American Poetry Review*
g. *Poetry*
h. *Kalliope*

Internet Magazine Sites (magazines without print versions):

a. *Able Muse*
b. *Adirondack Review*
c. *Can We Have Our Ball Back?*
d. *Drunken Boat*
e. *Ducts*
f. *Freshwater*
g. *MiPoesias*
h. *Mudlark*
i. *Pedestal*
j. *Rock*
k. *Salt Plum*
l. *Salt River Review*
m. *The Scream Online*
n. *Snakeskin*
o. *Tenemos*
p. *The Third Muse*
q. *The Third Muse* (Australia)
r. *Zone Magazine*
s. *Zuzu's Petals*

CHAPTER
5
ORCHESTRATING A COLLECTION

You've been writing for a while now, and you've had some good success in magazines. Does this mean you're ready for a book? Not necessarily. Though it's natural to want to go to the next level as soon as you have what you think amounts to critical mass, sometimes it's a mistake to do it. For instance, maybe you've published in lots of places, but deep down inside you know you haven't quite found your voice. In that case, wait. You've may have made great technical strides—and I'm betting you have—but don't try for a book yet. Hang on until it can be your book, and no one else's. Or maybe you've published lots of poems and you think they're all you, but their styles are all over the map. Don't do it then either, because it's critical that your new book be coherent—in fact, that's what we're going to spend this chapter talking about—so hold off until you've accumulated some good number of things that go together. Personally, I have hundreds of pages of published work that have never ended up in book form, not because I don't like the poems, but because, so far, they haven't happened to fit into any of my books.

You're a grownup. Be honest with yourself and if in your heart of hearts you don't think you're ready for a full-length collection yet for whatever reason, ignore that nagging voice—"But I'm thirty-three- forty-five-sixty-years old and I need to do this *now.*" It's a big mistake to publish something as permanent as a book if there's any chance you'll look back on it later and wish you hadn't. Besides, this afternoon, this month, this round of contests isn't your last opportunity, you know. If you aren't ready now, you will be. And how do I know that? Because you're here, and because I can tell you're the kind of person who keeps growing.

CHAPBOOKS IN GENERAL

If you have a lot of material around, but you've decided you haven't quite reached the book stage, maybe you're ready for a chapbook. In case you don't know, chapbooks are the middle ground between magazines and books. The difference between a chapbook and a book is length. "Book-length" implies a minimum of 48 pages of poetry, whereas chapbooks usually fall somewhere between 18 and 30 pages.

On the downside, chapbooks aren't usually as well-produced as books. This is partly because of the limited finances of most chapbook publishers and partly because, being so short, they can't have spines. Generally speaking, most chapbooks haven't gone to great aesthetic lengths with their covers, either. The exception to that is some letter press/small edition chapbooks, not often options offered to beginners, which are works of art in themselves and usually sell for a lot of money.

On the upside, if you do have a body of good, coherent work, you have nothing to lose by putting it into a chapbook, since you're free to re-use those poems when you're ready to publish something longer. And if you do start with a chapbook, you'll be in good company. Many very successful poets, people you'll have heard of, began their careers that way. If you look at the acknowledgment pages of books of poetry, you'll see that substantial parts of many of them will have appeared before in chapbook form.

Besides not standing to lose anything in the chapbook process, you may well gain some important practical advantages when it comes to publishing a book, which simply writing for and publishing in magazines can't offer. A chapbook of your poetry, especially if it's won a contest, will get your name into the public air and give you some personal, if limited, circulation. Also, the exercise of putting a chapbook manuscript together will have started you thinking in larger forms than single poems, which in turn will be a leg up when you are ready to do a book.

HOW TO PUT A CHAPBOOK TOGETHER

Now…pour yourself a cup of coffee and let's talk about how you might go about all this. The first thing to keep in mind is that any poems you're going to present as a group are going to need some clear reason to be keeping company. Other than the fact that they all happened to be waiting on the third floor when the elevator door opened, that is, or that they're all the poems you happened to write between 1970 and 1972. Those two sentences describe how a lot of chapbooks feel to me, but I'm hoping that when you do one, it won't turn out that way. What I'm trying to tell you here (and don't forget it, all right?) is that at the end of the day, the poems in any sequence—and your chapbook is a sequence—will need to flow from one to the other in a way that makes musical sense.

Decide Which Poems

Here's how you get started. First, sort through what you have and decide which poems are in and which are out. Keep only the ones you're sure of, setting the marginal ones aside, even if, conceptually, they seem to fit, until such time as you've reworked them. Use your own judgment as to what's marginal, though. Don't let the fact that a particular poem hasn't been published sway you. For instance, I was never able to place a poem of mine called "To Play Pianissimo" in a magazine, and not because I didn't try. But I put it into my chapbook anyway, and after that into my full-length collection of piano poems, because I liked it myself. As it turns out, "To Play Pianissimo" happens to be the poem out of all my piano pieces that people say is their favorite. In other words, I do really think that if you hold onto your private opinion about your work, once you've been around long enough to be able to trust your judgment, you'll be proved right in the end.

As you're going through the process of deciding which poems will be the lucky winners, keep two requirements in mind. The first I've already mentioned—you like the poems personally. The second—and I've implied that, too—is that, for one reason or another, you think they belong together.

Now it's easy to tell that poems can be profitably grouped when they have the same subject matter—a particular place, a time in your life, bicycles. But that's often not the case. So here are some other possibilities for you to think about. Maybe your poems have similar emotional centers. Maybe together they can travel from an old place to a new one. It isn't necessarily prohibitive that the poems you've chosen are in different styles. Maybe you can group them like a dance suite. Keep in mind, though, that since you don't have many pages to work with, a chapbook doesn't have as much room for experiment as a full-length book, and you can't get as organizationally complicated in it, either.

Find Your Theme

Okay, let's assume that you've now decided on a group of poems for your new collection. Your next step is to figure out why (keeping in mind that your "why" may not necessarily be linear) you chose these particular ones rather than others. Once you have it worked out, your "why" will tell you what the theme of your book is going to be. Good chapbooks—and this applies to full-length books, too—need themes, because if you don't know what your book's about, you can't weave the poems. And if you can't weave the poems, you can't make music.

Sometimes, at the end of the selection process, you'll find yourself left with a bunch of your efforts that, on the surface of it at least, don't seem much alike at all, even when you've thought of them in the ways I suggested just now. In that case, how would you go about articulating a theme? Well, if I asked you, "What do you want this chapbook to be about?" your answer would start you on the road. Sometimes just asking the question will make it pop right out. "It's all about desire," you say. Okay, that tells me a lot about how you'll want to build the poems. Or, it's about bicycles. Okay, but now we need to go farther. What do bicycles mean to you? You can try clustering if you like, the way I explained in the chapter about revision. Eventually, you'll reach something deeper than bicycles—like it's about being light in your bones and that's what it takes if you want to travel.

In other words, the theme of your chapbook may well not be your first thought when you've asked yourself the "What's-it-about?" question. You may have to go several layers deeper to reach your real answer. That's a good thing in itself, because in taking those steps, you'll be figuring out why you came. That in turn will be part of your answer to the question "Why am I alive?" And, of course, the more you can learn about that, the better, because what you know will reflect onto everything you do, the way the sun's center warms the earth.

Using Arcing To Work Out A Sequence

Once you've settled into your theme, however you got there—once you've moved in your new leather chairs, washed the windows, hung curtains—you'll be in a viable position to decide how to order your poems. Before this, you might as well have shuffled them and drawn them at random out of the deck.

By the way, there are poets who think books of poems *should* be arranged at random. I once heard a truly fine one advocate for this and argue against what I'm telling you now. So if you don't agree with me here, you're free to go elsewise and know that there are experienced people who agree with you. I think like a musician, though, and to me a book of poems is like a symphony and would benefit from being approached that way. So that's how I'm proceeding.

Once you've articulated your theme—or themes; even some chapbooks have more than one—ask yourself, "What kind of arc do I want for this book?" Every book, chap or not, needs to arc as it progresses from beginning to end, even if the arc looks like a fly trail or the progression of the kid around the neighborhood in a *Family Circus* cartoon. Ideally, it's the jet trail a piece of music leaves behind from the time it takes off until it lands safely at its destination. You could think of it, for instance, as the path of a plane that lifts off from blue Florida and lands in flooded Minnesota, where the sky's been grey so long it's changed the color of people's eyes.

Keeping the jet plane analogy for a minute, determining your arc is going to put you in the position of a trip planner, with your reader being the traveler. You decide where he/she starts, where she's going and how she'll get there. So, what kind of feeling do you want your reader to have as she climbs on the plane? Choose a poem that sets that up. That's the first poem of your chapbook. But there's a practical caveat, because here the analogy breaks down. Once a person is on a plane, like it or not, she has to sit through the flight. But your passenger can jump off at any time. What does that mean to your chapbook? It means that you'd better pick a really strong poem to start with or she may decide not to go at all.

So now you have poem number one. What's next? I think, before you can answer that question, you're going to have to decide exactly where you're going. So go back to the jet plane now, and visualize where you want your reader to land. What's the weather like? How do you want her to walk away feeling? Find another very strong poem that suits that, and put it at the end.

As you chose your first and last poems, you should have been thinking about your theme. Suppose it had been desire. Maybe you'd start with a flicker and end with a blaze. Or ash. Suppose it had been bicycles. Maybe you'd start with buying a bike and end with you being light enough to ride it. Or end with its disappearance into a sky, which is already full of bicycles. I don't know. Those aren't my books. But they do represent the way you're going to think.

Remember geometry? What do two points determine? Right: a line.

But poetry is a complex geometry, because in poetry the line between those two points may or may not be straight, depending on how you've ordered your poems.

The Mechanics of Arriving at Your Arc

There are lots of ways you can go about that. Here's one: write your titles on index cards. If you've listened to me, at this point your titles will reflect your poems, not be generic titles like "Ode" or "Song." Then set the cards out on a table and see if you can arrange them in such a way that, when you read through them, the titles make a poem. Keep in mind that to make your new "poem" work, you may have to take some cards out or reword others. Leave the cards there for several days, and read through them every time you happen to pass the table, changing the order if it feels wrong to you. Eventually, you'll end up with a sequence you don't any more feel the need to reconsider, and if you've titled your poems clearly, that sequence may work just as well for the whole poems as it did for their titles.

Alternatively, you might approach sequencing not just by titles but by whole poems. This approach requires some floor space. It's not practical if you live in a studio apartment or have dogs and cats. Lay your poems out on the floor, between the one that's first and the one that's last. Again, read through them, moving them around when the order feels wrong, until they all seem to stop someplace. Leave them to their own devices for a day or so, and if they still don't want to move when you come back, you'll have it.

If those approaches don't feel right to you, maybe this will. You want to imply that your chapbook is, at least in one way of looking at it, a single poem. So check the last line of your first poem, and find another whose first line could be a continuation of that. Then look at the last line of your second poem, and find the one whose first line keeps it moving. And so on. This approach probably won't work perfectly, because real life isn't so neat, but it can be a useful way of putting most of your manuscript together.

NAMING YOUR CHAPBOOK

Okay. You finally have everything the way you want it. Now it's time to think of an overall title. You may have had one in mind from the beginning, and that's fine, but before you settle on it, you need to make sure it still fits your manuscript. Most chapbooks/books go through a few incarnations (my collection *Hunger* had at least five, and *Torn* probably a dozen) before they settle, and sometimes the final version is all the way across the country from the one you started out with.

Actually, naming your book ahead of time can be a bit cart-before-the-horse, like documenting a program before you've written it. It's old wisdom in computer circles that documentation (commenting) is always best done afterwards, because though you know in advance what you want the program to do, you seldom know exactly how you're going to make it do that. You may think you know, but the bugs you get yourself into when you actually sit down to write the code will show you otherwise.

Another way to think about pre-titles is that they amount to naming your baby before she/he's born. People do that, but personally, I didn't feel comfortable giving my children names until I saw what they looked like.

I don't want to sound bombastic about this. I'm not saying that deciding on a title ahead of time is always a bad idea—it can be, for instance, a focal point when you sit down to arrange your poems. I just want to be sure that you don't keep it out of hand but check back once you're finished, to be sure it suits the way you've ended up.

No matter how you arrive at it, even setting aside what we hope will be its resonance with your poems, you need to understand that your choice of title will have practical consequences. It can make someone pick your book up from a rack. Alternatively, it can cause a browser in the store to slur right over it. Some titles sound generic; others make you think of textbooks. Others, though, can attract attention because they have emotional thrust or draw a browser to take a second look because they're strange.

Here are some things to consider. One-word titles can be easy to remember, but you have to be careful to avoid words that have any taint of cliché. Also, if you use a one-word title, there's always the chance that someone has already written a book by that name. There have been at least three books called *Hunger,* for instance. I found that out after the fact. The first one seems to have been a nonfiction book, which came out in the 1930s.

Very long titles can pique interest, and because you have so many words to work with, you can get very specific, so there's no chance anyone can confuse your book with any other. Titles in the middle, on the other hand, are pretty common, so they're going to have to fend for themselves. If you are looking at two-or-three word titles, try to come up with something unusual. Otherwise, someone looking at a shelf of books with titles of similar lengths won't be drawn to yours.

Be sure you don't accidentally call your book anything an antagonistic reviewer can use to make fun of you. One of the earliest versions of *Hunger* was organized by the Dewey decimal system. I called this manuscript *Shelf Life*. I thought that was a pretty clever title until a friend pointed out to me what a reviewer who didn't like the book could do with it. Actually, the whole idea was a little too clever (read "pretentious") in the first place, too many wheels within wheels, so it wasn't hard to abandon it.

Here's what I think. A really good title is always bigger than the book it names. It can't be too confined in its implications because, like a rocket ship on a launch pad, it's going to need maximum metaphoric thrust. In other words, it should allow your reader to envision not just one thing, the subject of one of your poems, for example, but so many things that a place can be found for it in his/her life now, right here in the bookstore or the library.

HOW ASSEMBLING A FULL-LENGTH COLLECTION IS DIFFERENT

Everything I've said about putting a chapbook together can be applied to full-length manuscripts, except that when you do a whole book, you'll find that your unit will be the section rather than the poem. Chapbooks don't usually have sections, but full-length books almost always do. In some respects, the sections of your new manuscript will amount to little chapbooks, but you can't consider them in isolation, because they're going to have to talk to each other across section lines. Because of this, the ordering of poems within your full-length collection may be completely different from the sequencing of those same poems in the chapbooks they came from.

Here's what you know so far: with a chapbook, poems will talk to each other across pages. In a full-length book this also happens, but what's different now is that whole sections are being set off against each other, and they are also, naturally, going to call back and forth. So you may, depending on what your collection is like, want to get clear on what the theme of each section is before you decide on a final order.

A CASE STUDY

I'll give you an example of this. In 1989, I published a chapbook called *Across Her Broad Lap Something Wonderful,* and a few years later wanted to use most of it again, as part of a manuscript I was putting together, which after many incarnations evolved into *Hunger.* I tried putting the poems from *Across Her Broad Lap* into *Hunger* in the sequence they were already in. But they just weren't happy like that, so I took them apart and started over.

The theme of *Across Her Broad Lap* had been the emotions underlying a relationship between two people. It began with "To Play Pianissimo," in which an important secret is communicated. Then it moved from one person's need for another (the secret) to love, to passion, to disillusion, and ended with a sort of joy as these two people flowed together, two very different rivers becoming one. The first line of the book was, "To play pianissimo does not mean silence." In other words, something is about to open. The last was, "Across her broad lap, something wonderful begins," leaving the rivers flowing outwards towards the sea. I intended those first and last lines to frame the story I wanted to tell.

But *Hunger* was a different animal. It was one of those cases of apparently unrelated poems having come together. The reason I'd decided to put those poems in the same book, my "why," took me a while to fathom; in fact, it took me several years. Once I'd figured it out, though, it was perfectly clear. Every one of the surviving poems was, in one way or another, about hunger. And not just any hunger. When I burrowed deeper, I found out that what I was meaning by hunger wasn't the kind that can kill us, but specifically the kind that keeps us alive. The hunger in my book is my lifelong passion for something I can't name—and I'm not sure, word-oriented though I am, that I even want to know its name. It's this hunger that keeps me moving forward in my life. If I ever satisfied it, I really think that I might as well lie down and go to sleep forever.

So as you can see, since the sequencing of the poems in *Hunger* was meant to have a completely different arc from the one they'd described in *Across Her Broad Lap,* of course the old way didn't work any more. And, besides that, once I'd figured out my theme, I saw that a few of the poems from *Across Her Broad Lap,* and "To Play Pianissimo" was one of them, didn't belong in *Hunger* at all. So I deleted those, and I started working on ordering the rest, and some newer poems. I decided to begin inwardly with myself and work outwards into the world. By the end of the book I'd arrived at the sky.

Now if you happen to have read *Hunger*, you'll know that its progression isn't really as linear as I've been implying. The truth is I couldn't tell you, probably, exactly why certain poems are where they are. All I can say is that they just felt right there. You won't be able to explain why each and every poem in your own book is where it is either, and that's okay. What I've been trying to give you is a feeling for how to begin arranging the story you came to tell.

USING MUSIC TO THINK ABOUT COLLECTIONS

Many of the books of poems I like as books can be imagined as musical wholes. When I wrote *Forty-Four Ambitions for the Piano*, I tried to spell that literally out by using one line of a Bach Sarabande to begin each section, so that when you'd played through the section heads, you'd have played the Sarabande, and therefore the book.

In fact, try using musical metaphors to help you figure out the arc you want your poems to describe. For instance, it might be useful to think of your new book as if you'd composed a symphony. If you read up on symphonic structure, you can broaden your appreciation of music as well as learn about organizational principles you may not have thought of. Or, and this will make your work come out differently than if you were using the symphonic model, you might think of your book as a concert. Well-planned concerts almost always offer more variety of style than symphonies. They may also often start simple and work up to more challenging material, and they'll vary the pace by putting short pieces in to rest the audience by breaking up what might otherwise be an unrelievedly intense listening sequence.

On Rests

Related to this last point, one thing to consider when you're working on a whole book is that you need to give the reader someplace to sit. He or she's going through this series of poetry masterworks (we hope so, anyway) and at some point s/he'll get tired of concentrating. So let her relax a minute by giving her simple poems, gentle poems, humorous poems. These can work as little silences in your book, serving the same function as rests in music.

Now with a book as with a chapbook, you want to start and end strong, and you want to be sure your first and last poems make an appropriate frame for what you're trying to do. But whereas in a chapbook there's no room for anything you aren't positive of, in a full-length book you're justified in using non-blockbuster poems to serve as the rests I was talking about a minute ago. You're also justified in using experimental work which, because it is experimental, you should put somewhere in the middle. You don't want your reader to end up with an atypical piece as her sole idea of who you are, and if you put experimental stuff at the beginning, the reader will obviously be misled as to how you usually write. In fact, I think that experimental work in a longer book is even a good idea, because it shows the poet is still learning. And it can be stimulating for a reader who may have settled into his/her expectation that the rest of the book is going to be exactly however it's been so far. On the other hand, don't overdo it. Use your odder stuff judiciously. If it's only a little odd, you can use it like salt. But if it's really really odd, maybe it's more like habañeras—those orange lanterns that can burn the back of your throat so you don't want any more hot food again ever—put it in here and there, and leave it at that.

On Accidentals

Here's something else to think about. It can be interesting not to put every single poem that belongs to a group into the same section of your finished manuscript. If you move one of these poems out, something nice can happen. When your reader gets to the relocated poem, it will draw him/her back to its relatives in the earlier section. Using echoing like this has several potential benefits. It will help a reader internalize, if she hasn't already, the fact that your book is woven and not strictly linear. It may also leave him/her with a deeper understanding of your earlier section, by putting its concerns in a new context. And, by creating a little intentional dissonance in the later section, you'll have made the reader think, "Hm-m, why did she put this in here?" No matter what conclusion she or he draws, this pause for reflection is bound to involve him/her more deeply with you than before.

OTHER METAPHORICAL APPROACHES

Obviously, music isn't the only way to think about putting your book together. There are probably as many ways as there are books. But since I've used music a lot myself, I brought it up first. Alternatively, you might think of your work as if it were fiction—buildup, conflict, resolution, dénouement. Or, you could take a pre-existing structure such as a church service, a baseball game, a cookbook, an appointment book, and use that as your framework.

ON CONSIDERING THE READER

It's easy to forget about the reader when you decide to put your work in any form out into the world at large. Of course, you've been writing to express your own personal self. That's how it should be, and we've spent a lot of time talking about how great it is, and how it can help you live a fuller and more personal life. And for sure, if you don't get deeply, personally full-frontally involved in what you're writing, then sooner or later someone will notice you're either hiding or you're a phony. *But.* When you decide you want to publish what you've written, then by definition it isn't only you.

So you're going to want to arrange your poems with some thought of a reader. When you've finished assembling your manuscript, read it from the beginning, pretending as best you can that you've never seen it before, and see how it strikes you. Because this is what your reader will be doing.

But don't get obsessed. You have no obligation—in fact it's silly to try—to reach every imaginable reader. One of the most profound things my father ever told me, and he came to it because at the time I was running around trying to please, was "Listen, Lo. No matter what you do, there are going to be people who will hate your guts." Once I really believed him, I stopped trying to be what I thought other people might like and just did what my insides told me was right for me. This applies to you, too. Write what you know is most true. Arrange it in a true way. And when you're finished, you'll find there will be people who will actively dislike your book, people who won't even finish it. But there will also be people who will travel with you. Those people will be your true soul-mates, because you weren't lying, either in the poems or in the way you put them together. So what your reader saw wasn't your idea of what poems, or a book, should be, it wasn't your "A" paper, wasn't even your MFA. What your reader saw was you.

EXERCISES
Making Arrangements

1. Find a chapbook by someone whose work you like. Read it several times and see if you can work out why the poems are sequenced as they are. Since not every poet is good at sequencing, you may not be able to come up with a connecting principle; if you can't, that in itself is useful information. Now, photocopy the whole chapbook. Sit down with the pages and arrange them for yourself, at least two of the ways we talked about—for instance, by having the last line of one poem lead to first line of the next, by theme, etc. While you're at it, see if you think there are any poems which, because they don't fit or because they're weak, shouldn't have been included.

2. Find a book by someone whose work you like. Start by analyzing the sections as if each section were a chapbook. When you have the section principles worked out in your mind, look at the way the sections are ordered within the book, which of course determines how the book moves between the beginning and the end. Remember, the book may come back in on itself or it may not. Also remember that the poet may not have been a good organizer. Now, photocopy the book and sit down with the pieces. Are there poems you'd move from one section to another? Are there poems you think should have been cut? Arrange the finished sections in at least two ways. Think about how the book's impact would change if the poet had used each of them. Something that might be interesting to try: see what would happen if the order of the poems in the book had been exactly reversed.

CHAPTER

6

OUT LOUD

HOW NOT TO DO A POETRY READING

You'd think that the most profound way to receive a poem would be to be lucky enough to hear the poet himself/herself read it for you. But if you've been to many poetry readings, you'll have noticed that lots of poets don't do justice to their own work. Some mumble, to the point where you can hardly catch what they're saying. Others present poems, which ought to sound passionate, in tiny, mousy voices. Others read everything in one unvarying cadence, while carefully raising the pitch at the end of each line. Still others drone on and on, as if they were poetry bagpipes. At the opposite extreme of the expressiveness scale are the speech-teacher poets who declaim their work, complete with hand gestures. I once saw a highly acclaimed poet, whose delicate poetry I love, do that to the point where I wanted to jump up on the stage and pull him off with one of those canes they used to use in vaudeville.

There are other ways to ruin a reading too, lots of them. But I want to mention one more. Some poets, maybe because they're shy and trying to avoid getting to the personal, maybe because they're arrogant, are given to such long introductions that by the time they actually do arrive at the poem you don't care any more. I actually walked out of a reading recently (I almost never do that) because three times in a row the poet told seemingly interminable stories about her genealogical research as introductions to very very short poems, which she read with no enthusiasm whatsoever. This poet happens to be very famous, and I admire her poetry a lot, but I have to say that her reading diminished my opinion of her because either she didn't care about the audience, or she didn't care about her own work. In fact, the atmosphere of abuse in the room, of her audience or of the poems, it doesn't really matter which, was what pushed me to the point that I left.

Etiquette-wise, leaving isn't usually an option. I would never have done it even in this case had the audience not been enormous and the poet famous enough not to need me there. As a rule, whether you like what a fellow writer is presenting or not, you should never leave unless the circumstances are that extreme and you're positive there's no chance the reader's feelings would be hurt. That's basic courtesy and something we all owe each other as poets.

How to Get Started and Do Better

What I'd like to do in this chapter is to rescue you from giving the sorts of sometimes tedious, sometimes excruciating readings I've been describing, and I'm going to do that by telling you how you can present your poems to their absolutely best advantage. You may never read even one poem in public let alone give a whole reading. But if you decide to try to publish your work, and if you're successful at it, sooner or later you're almost going to have to stand up in front of a group, because readings are one important way we poets get our writing out in the world. And if you're lucky, an audience who's liked what it heard will be moved enough to take your poem (and/or your books) home.

This information is going to be important to you even if you never read your poetry in a public setting (you may not want to, and that's fine), because even then, at some point if you keep on writing, you'll find yourself reading something out loud to someone—be it a friend, your mother, your lover, or your twelve-year-old niece. And when you do that, everything I'm about to tell you about presenting poems is going to apply.

Venues: On Slams

To begin with, and here I'm addressing this to those of you who may want to get public, let me tell you a little about organized venues. You've probably heard of poetry slams, which have gotten really popular in the last few years. Slams don't appeal to me personally, for a couple of reasons. First of all, I'm uncomfortable with anything that turns poetry into a sporting event. And that's what a slam does. Because it's a competition, there are winners and, by implication, losers, and since I don't think anyone who writes poetry is a loser, I don't like that implication.

The second reason I don't recommend slams for those of you reading this book is that they, and performance poetry in general, seem to me to belong to a specifically oral tradition, whereas what we've been talking about here in *Feathers* is how to put words on paper. Don't get me wrong. I'm not saying slams can't be gripping experiences. I'm just saying that they aren't, at the moment, us.

My reason for this is that I think that though some words on paper have the potential to work well out loud, in my experience the converse isn't usually true. From what I've seen, very few performance poems hold their own on the page. I'm well aware that even if I'm right in general, there are exceptions, but since I'm the one who's writing this book, I have to go from where I am, and that's where I am.

VENUES OTHER THAN SLAMS

So, slams aside, here's how you might find healthy-to-you places to read. If you live in a medium-sized town or in a city, your local arts newspaper will list upcoming readings. To begin with, look for coffee houses that have open mike nights where anyone can come and do a poem or two. The big advantage of coffee houses, and places like them, is that because all the poets are amateurs they aren't, at least not overtly, competing with each other, so the atmosphere is usually supportive. A reasonable way to start on this track would be to go and lurk for a night or so, then when you're ready, take a friend along for moral support, breath deeply a few times, and put your name down on the list.

Besides coffee houses, some bookstores arrange readings for groups of local writers. And there are all sorts of miscellaneous reading venues, too. After you've gotten experience with open mikes, you'll probably find yourself invited to read your work with only one other person or by yourself. At that point, you'll have arrived as a reader.

A SIDEBAR ON MICROPHONES

If you do much talking in public, sooner or later you'll find a microphone in front of you. Mikes, if you don't know how to use them, can definitely undermine you. Beginners get too close and every time they say "p," the sound makes a pop. Or they get restless and move their heads around and the poems fade in and out. Or they sound muffled because they don't understand distance. Or they don't realize that the mike will pick everything up, so every time they rattle a page it comes across.

Here's what you need to know about mikes. There are two basic kinds: unidirectional and onmidirectional. Unidirectional mikes have sweet spots like tennis rackets. You want to find out where that is and speak into it. With omnidirectional mikes, the whole surface of the mike picks up sound. This means that they may pick up more than your voice, so be careful of rattling papers.

There are different ways you can be miked. Sometimes the mike is on a gooseneck fixed to a podium. Personally, I hate that because I like to move around and when I use a fixed mike I end up with a stiff neck from hovering over it. Sometimes it's on a stand, but you can take it off. When you do that, the mike becomes a hand-held mike. Sometimes, you wear it on your lapel with a receiver clipped somewhere on your body. That's what newscasters do, and it's called a lavalier mike. Sometimes, and this applies mostly to the stage, it's taped, usually to your cheek where it hovers like an insect, just in your peripheral vision.

Here's how to handle the various kinds. If it's fixed, you'll just need to lean over it. If it's on a stand, don't set it right in front of your lips; set it an inch or so below. If you don't, you'll have to stretch your neck to read into it, which will thin your voice. If you take the mike off the stand, be careful not to swing it away from yourself, because this will cause your voice to fade in and out. If you're wearing it, in other words, it's a lavalier, speak in its general direction, and if you turn, turn your whole body, not just your head.

It helps to know what the mike will do ahead of time, so if you can, be sure to do a sound check before the reading starts. When you do, say "Peter Piper picked a peck of pickled peppers," or words to that effect, because that will tell you how close you can get without popping your "p's." If you can't do an overt sound check, then do a covert one once you get up there.

By the way, you may have noticed how rock stars look like they're eating their mikes. That's because the closer you get to the mike, the richer and fuller you'll sound, and conversely, the farther away, the thinner you'll come off. The best posture in front of a mike, sound-wise, is a slightly lowered head. Don't forget to look at the audience, though. Reading out loud is communication, after all, and your eyes will add to that.

On Nerves

There's no question that when you stand up for the first time to read poems to an audience, it's not going to feel anonymous. The feedback is immediate, and there's nowhere to hide, no way to pretend that someone else wrote this stuff. Self-exposure in a situation like this can be a frightening experience. Your voice will tend to shake. You'll probably read too fast. You'll more than likely drop your papers on the floor and have to go down on your hands and knees looking for them. You'll almost certainly be tempted to get up and apologize for yourself covertly or overtly before you start speaking, no matter how much, if you have any sense, you know you shouldn't. Don't worry. It gets better.

But "better" may be only relative because, for some people, familiarity never quite beats down that initial nervousness. If your fear of standing in front of a group doesn't go away with time, though, it doesn't mean you aren't cut out to be in public. Many actors, people whose names you'd recognize, have stage fright. They just go through it, and so can you.

They say if you have stage fright, you should imagine your audience naked. That doesn't work for me. Here are some things you can try instead. They're listed in chronological order, because planning a reading is a little like planning a wedding.

A week before the reading, make a list of the worst things that could happen, then act out each of them. If you think you'll drop your papers, stand up as if you were reading, then do it. If you think you'll read too fast, do it. If you tend towards "ums," try injecting one after every sentence. This will get those kinds of events out of your system.

On the day of your reading, drink a lot of water and avoid dairy products and caffeine, because those can cause phlegm. If you think you're losing your voice, eat a lemon. An old jazz singer told me about that once and it really works. Years ago my husband and I sang in nightclubs. One night I got to the gig with absolutely no voice; I could only croak. I ate a whole lemon and my voice came completely back long enough to do two sets.

As you're sitting in the audience waiting to be introduced, calm yourself down by doing one or more of the following: 1) Count backwards 20 to 1, one breath for each number, each breath deeper; 2) Visualize a nice warm soft place; 3) Imagine swallowing your favorite food; do this several times; 4) Feel your head floating up towards the ceiling; 5) Imagine weights on the corners of your jaw, and feel it drop; 6) Drop your shoulders, then imagine them weightless; 7) Breathe—relaxation in, tension out.

Remember to keep breathing during your reading. If you don't, somewhere in the middle you may find your jitters returning. If you start choking up, bite the edges of your tongue; this suppresses phlegm. If, instead, your mouth gets dry, biting the tip of your tongue will produce saliva. But it's better to avoid all this by breathing, deeply and slowly.

CHOOSING WHAT TO READ AT OPEN MIKES

Not all poems work equally well in the air. You'll have in your portfolio poems that shine on the page but are too complicated to be susceptible to understanding on one hearing. On the other hand, you'll find that you have others that may or may not be as strong as those, but have undeniable emotional impact when read out loud. Now what I mean by "not your strongest" poems isn't stuff that may be sentimental schlock, but rather poems that are simple in their conceptions. Because of these poems' simplicity, you may not be as fond of them as you are of others that it took more parts of you to make, but if you're reading only a poem or two, I'd advise you to go for the accessible. You'll have to if you want to succeed, because you won't have enough time to build up support for your favorite deeper poems.

Never read a poem in public that you aren't happy with. Some people get up and say, "Well, I wrote this poem this afternoon, it just came out, let's see how it goes." I've seen even established poets do something like that, but I think it's a mistake, because it leaves us with the impression that you're not giving us your best. Your best, I think, is something you owe us as an audience. It's a matter of mutual respect.

ORCHESTRATING A FULL-LENGTH READING

So far we've been talking as if you were just starting out, in which case you'll be one of several readers and do three poems at the most each time. Now we'll move on to how you might put a program together when you're asked to do a whole reading by yourself.

The first thing you'll need to understand is that organizing poems for a reading is completely different from organizing them in book form. When you're putting a manuscript together, you should always start with something really strong. You don't want the reader, who at this point is functioning as a kind of judge, to put that book down. But when you're doing a reading, a "wow" poem probably isn't the best way to begin, because your audience won't know you yet. You want to get them used to the sound of your voice first. To make that happen, you should begin your reading with something you like, something accessible. If you don't, you run the risk of immediately narrowing your audience down to those few people (and they will be few) who read a lot of poetry and can appreciate the finer points of your more complicated poems. Wait until the middle for those, because by then the nonreaders in your audience will probably like you so much they won't mind not overtly "getting" some of your work. Besides, you'll have to warm up too. It's likely to take you the first couple of poems to get rid of any unsettled feelings you may have had when you walked up to the front of the room and turned around to see that everyone was waiting for you.

So, start simple. Also, end simple. You want to leave people with a clear impression of you, something to take home. If you happen to have written a poem that you know has a lot of emotional impact, especially if it's good emotion, do it last. And don't forget to leave the moment of silence before you say thank you and get off the stage.

The middle of your reading is a more complicated question. It will help if you think of a reading as a concert. A concert needs variety, but it can't shift moods too abruptly, and the reason this won't work is simple—audiences can't do that. They need some time. Now, when you're arranging a book, you can do the shifting complexly. For instance, in a book you may want to spread closely related poems out so they can talk to each other across the pages. But this approach won't work at all in the case of a reading. In fact, it's almost guaranteed to fail, because by the time you've reached the second of your linked poems, your audience will have, to all intents and purposes, forgotten the first. So if you do have poems that belong together, you should perform them together. And make it clear from your introduction to the first one that the next several poems belong to the same mindset.

Any time you've put your audience through an emotional wringer during your reading, be sure to build in a chance to relax. Humorous poems are good for this. I have a few, but not many, so instead I tend to use my links or simple poems for tension reduction, the kind of poems whose impact I hope is the beauty of what I'm describing. I intend those poems as sighs.

Putting all this together, here's the bottom line. Give your reading/ concert an arc by starting simply, then building to your highest level of complexity. Then build back down, realizing that your last poem doesn't function at all the same way as the first. The first (as we've discussed) should be a get-into-the-sound-of-my-voice poem. The last, because it can assume the voice is there now (either it is or it isn't, right?) should be a "wow" poem, but not a technical one, an emotional "wow" poem. Save the technical "wow" poems for the middle.

TIME YOUR READING

You should never read for more than your allotted time, so as soon as you've chosen your poems, unless you've done lots of readings before, you should time them, then total them. (You can allow a minute to a minute and a half for introductions.) Your total shouldn't be over 45 minutes. That's about the longest you can expect an audience to listen carefully. Keep in mind that it's always better to leave them wanting more than to go on too long. If you do that, they'll start getting tired, and if you go on way too long, that will be the main thing they'll remember about you, no matter how good your poems were. And never ask your listeners, do you mind if I read three more poems? They may say they don't mind, but more likely than not, they'll feel manipulated into agreeing and they'll hold it against you.

It's a good idea to warn the audience when you're about two poems from the end. If you don't do that, they're going to get more and more distracted, wondering how much longer you're going to be. By telling them, "These are the last two poems" or "I'm just going to read two more," you can assure they'll really be listening, and especially listening when it comes to the last one, which, if you've chosen thoughtfully, will be the perfect place to leave them. What you should never do is say, "I'm going to read two more poems," then read three. Two, and that's it, thank you so much for coming, good night.

USE LINKS WELL

Some people do this, but don't you: title, poem, title, poem, title, poem, title, poem, sit down. This approach ignores the fact that no one hearing poems for the first time—not me, not anyone—is likely to "get" everything you intended them to get. So it's critical that you help your listeners out all you can, by telling them in advance anything you think would be useful for them to know. Besides, if you do that, you'll be giving them, besides information, a sense of you personally. This is a big thing. If you've shared something of yourself before you read, then you'll be likely to have everyone in the room on your side before you've even started the poem. And believe me, from up front you can tell when an audience is on your side. Knowing they are will help you relax, and when you're relaxed, you'll be sure to read better.

RESPECT YOUR AUDIENCE

When you think about it, it's simple. If you obviously care about your listeners—you help them out, you're yourself in front of them—then they're going to care about you. If, on the other hand, you obviously don't—you patronize them, you give the impression of wanting to get it over with, or, you won't get off the stage, then why should they feel any obligation? The hard truth is that this applies also to the case where the reason you didn't say anything before you read that poem was that you were too shy. Your listeners probably won't dislike you, but they won't have any advance reason to be positive, either.

Here are some ideas for introducing your work. Tell people how you came to write this particular poem. Audiences are always interested in that, especially if they're made up mostly of people who don't write. Tell them what you think the poem's about. I know I've said you need to trust the reader and not spell out what you mean, but in this case it's fine to do that, because though your poem's intent or situation may be perfectly clear to someone who has the chance to sit down and take time with it, at a reading, if you care that your listeners get your particular point, you'll need to tell them what to listen for. In some cases, the ostensible moral of your poem may not matter to you. Instead, what you may care most about is its emotional impact. If that's so, then don't mention meaning at all, or reassure the audience that whatever they get out of this poem is fine with you.

If your poem happens to contain any foreign words or private references, be sure to translate them first. If you do, then your audience will feel in on your secrets. If you don't, they'll feel pushed away.

Don't hold back in any of this. People will be interested in what you have to say. Definitely, they will. I think only in rare cases, as for instance when you're reading several very short pieces in a row, should you not introduce each one. On the other hand, remember not to make the mistake that famous poet did and talk self-indulgently long. After all the poems are the reason you're here, not the introductions. In an open-mike situation especially, long introductions will make you look greedy, and your fellow poets who are waiting for their turns will resent you.

Introductions are important in another way, too, one I haven't mentioned yet. Introducing what you're about to read, besides being useful in itself, gives your audience a chance to breathe. As you know, poetry is compressed. That's one reason it isn't prose. Asking an audience to concentrate fiercely on several poems in a row is unrealistic and unfair. That's why sophisticated cooks often serve something light between courses, such as sherbet, to refresh the palate.

So, since one point of your introductions is going to be their function as sherbet, if, and only if, it happens to come easily to you, it's not a bad idea to digress a little as you go, or to tell a story with some humor in it, always keeping in mind that you want to keep its length under control.

One more general point about introductions: After the first, which of course you'll start as soon as you're settled at the mike, don't leap into them too fast. As a beginner, you'll tend to do that, because subconsciously you'll want to get your reading over with and sit down. Even when you've had experience you can still, inadvertently, make this mistake—or at least I used to—because you're so busy thinking ahead. But you should never forget that some of our most profound communications happen in silence, and that each poem you read needs its own moment afterwards, so that your listeners can have time to take it in. Respect that moment. Let each poem have its own following stillness, like a wake after its boat. Then go on.

GOOD DELIVERY

Don't Say "Uh"

At first, if you're not used to standing up in front of groups, you find your voice sounding unnatural to you, as if you were hearing yourself on tape for the first time. After a while you'll get used to that and also better at being yourself in what you say. Even so, though, you may have distracting vocal habits or intonations that will take away from your words, no matter how wonderful they may be. I did a reading a few years ago, which was taped by my local NPR station. I'd done radio before, in England and in the U.S., and had also read poems in the course of taped interviews, but this was the first time I'd heard a whole reading. I was horrified to hear that my introductions were often punctuated with burps—"Uh…uh…uh." They sounded awful. The next time I read for an audience, I listened to myself and found out that the recording hadn't been an aberration. I did it all the time. When I thought it over, I figured out that I'd been using "uhs" to buy time while I decided what to say next. Once I got that far, I began to notice that people who are interviewed a lot don't say anything, until they know what to say. Sometimes there are even a few seconds of complete silence. Keep in mind that those silences don't make them sound indecisive. They make them sound wise. In fact, John Wayne's strong and silent reputation may have been due to the fact that, according to him, he had only one acting technique. He counted to three before each line.

In other words, the way to combat stumbling is to consciously convert whatever your version of "uh's" is—and if you don't know, get someone to tape you—to silence. If you do that, you'll find your voice will flow like a river without snags, from one sentence to the next.

Read Slowly

Of course, what I've just said doesn't apply to the poems themselves, because the words for those are settled in advance. Still, for other reasons, I think you may need some extra coaching to do your poems really well and in your own way. One critical thing, something everyone will tell you and probably someone already has, is to read them slowly. Think about molasses. Pretend you're walking towards the deep end of a swimming pool full of Jell-o. When you're starting out, if what you're reading sounds excruciatingly slow to you, you'll probably have it about right. If you have any doubt about the disadvantages of fast, or even normal speed, reading, think about how hard it is sometimes to make out certain song lyrics, even when you really want to learn them. Both singers and poets sometimes deliver words too fast for comprehension, because they know what's coming next. But their listeners don't. Besides, especially in the case of poetry, words should be tasted, not bolted. When you've read out loud a lot, a speed that will have seemed crazily slow to you at first will become natural.

Practice Ahead of Time

While we're on the subject of reading out loud, performing a poem should never be the first time you've thought of it *viva voce*. You should have been saying it over and over *out loud* while you were working on it, even if you weren't planning to do it in public—which you legitimately might not have been, because not every good poem works well for readings. So if you aren't going to read this poem out loud, why should you do it when you're writing it? Because the music the words made when they're spoken (read "sung") should have been part of the reason they were chosen for the poem in the first place. That music is sometimes hard to see on the page, the way fabric is sometimes hard to see as a dress, even when you're experienced at sewing. People who've thought about their poems out loud are obvious when they read. They're the ones who know where the musical stresses fall. They're the ones who get it right.

Take notice of what radio newspeople do. They make dull sentences sound interesting all the time. You, with your not-dull poetry, can make it sound enthralling. It's all a matter of practice. When you're getting ready for a reading, I'd advise you to plan ahead. Experiment with different stresses. Vary your pace. Think about where the breaths are. Do each poem over and over until it feels natural in your mouth and you find you're telling it the same way every time. You don't want to get up there and look down at the page and then on the spot try to figure out how it might go.

Practicing is also a good idea, because it will force you to give each poem personal consideration. It's especially important that you not do every one in exactly the same way as every other one. After all, do you want your poems to come off as grown daughters dolled up in matching outfits, right down to the colors of their hair ribbons?

Avoid the "MFA Reading Style"

There's a very specific reading style some poets who've been through writing programs have picked up. If you go to enough readings, you'll be sure to hear it. Listen for a "poetry voice" and a rising cadence at the end of each line, which trails off at the end as if, no matter what it actually says, the line were a profound question. There are some fine poets who, in my opinion, have done themselves a great disservice by buying into this. Their work on the page is distinctive, but you'd never know it, because when they read they all sound alike.

Try Memorizing

There's something else you might consider doing when you're thinking about presenting your poetry out loud to best advantage. And that is (don't faint) telling your poems from memory. A reading, like a play, isn't one-way. It's a matter of communion between poet and audience. There has to be rapport, or no matter how good a poet's work is, it won't succeed. You'll find that most poets read from the page, and that's okay. You can do that, and after you've done the same poems a few times, you'll begin to feel safe enough to look up between lines.

The main trouble with reading from the page, though, is that when you do that, there will always be the book or your folder between you and your audience. It's true that the folder or book is safety, it's something to hide behind, and, true that with it you feel more stable than you otherwise would. But there's no way around it—it's also a barrier.

I used to read from the page. But one night, a long time ago now, I was in the middle of a reading and found I really, really wanted to read a certain poem I hadn't brought with me. Well, my first thought was, "What a shame I can't do that." Then I realized I knew the poem by heart, and, because I really did want to read it, I tried. And it worked.

When I got home, I thought about it and realized that the atmosphere in the room had changed when I stopped reading—that when I just said the poem, the audience was with me in a way it hadn't been before. "So why was that?" I wondered. Well, for one thing, because I didn't have the book in my hands for that one poem, I found I could look at my listeners one person at a time, and when I did that, I felt the kinship between myself and them. When I felt that kinship, I wasn't alone any more. Of course, the reward that time came at a price, because reciting that poem felt like walking a tightrope without a net, since if I'd forgotten the words, I'd have had nothing to fall back on.

Then I realized something else, which was that actually I know all my poems. So, theoretically, I hadn't needed the books in the first place. I tried it out on my next reading. I brought cheat-sheets to the podium with me, just in case. It turned out I never looked at them. Now I go up bare-handed, and I find my readings more rewarding than they were before. It's not that I don't notice that I'm standing up there naked; it's that I usually feel that my audience is more with me than they were when I was hiding behind the books.

Besides...I believe in the power of poetry: Yeats', Merwin's, mine or yours or anyone else's—and reading from memory is a way of standing right up in front of God and everyone and saying so. Now that I don't need the books any more, I've been able to come out from behind the podium—which, when you think about it, implied I was a teacher, whereas in fact I was only ever one of us.

You may be thinking you couldn't possibly do that. Sure you could. Can you sing songs from memory? I'll bet you can. Do you still remember advertising jingles from when you were a kid? Sure you do. So there's no reason you can't memorize your own poems. You might have to put a little effort into it. I admit, I've never consciously memorized mine; I just know them from working on them so hard for so long—but take it from me, it will be worth it. But you know what? If you decide not to try memory, if you just read your poems off the page for your whole life, more power to you for doing it at all, and don't worry about it.

EXERCISES
Practicing Out Loud

1. Pick ten poems you like by other people. Try to have as much variety as you can, in diction, in tone, in line length. Read them out loud. Then, think about what you could do better and try them again. Finally, tape yourself reading them and, when you listen to the tape, think how you could improve what you've just done. Do them once more, and listen.

2. From your own poems, draw up three different reading lists. Think about the emotions you're invoking. Think about the arc. Try to have the readings be as different from each other as you can.

3. Choose a theme that interests you in your work. Then, from your own poems, draw up a reading list that reflects that theme.

4. Make a list of your ten most accessible poems. Make a list of ten you like but you think won't work in the air. Consider why not.

5. Try to imagine when you read out loud that you're really singing. Does this change your voice?

6. From exercise 2 or 3, imagine how you would introduce each poem. Then, practice the reading as in exercise 1. Then try it out on a friend.

SECTION TWO
CONSIDERATIONS

CHAPTER
7
IN THE PARTICULAR

ON DETAIL

We think of poetry, as opposed to prose, as being about the big emotions, and often it is. But to write a good poem you have to understand a fact of psychology. Emotions always have contexts. You weren't in love by yourself, there was someone else involved, and that person had particular hair, feet, skin and maybe a tattoo of a snake on one breast. Or maybe he or she had one blue eye and one brown, or an odor in the crook of the arm that drove you crazy. What is it that brings him/her back to you now? The smoky sleeve of steam rising off a cup of lapsong? The sticky purple smell of the petunias in her front garden? The memory of his oar passing you the water bottle from the back of the canoe?

Loneliness isn't ever generic either. It always has a place, always weather. For instance, maybe it was raining last week, gray as thousands of falling mice. The silent phone on your hall table wouldn't stop screaming. When you couldn't stand it a second longer, you picked up your bird-head umbrella from its Chinese urn by the door and went out into the streets, turning right, then left, then who knew where. Everyone you passed seemed to have somewhere to go. You said "Good morning" to a man coming towards you under his scalloped water curtain, because you wanted to touch something, and because he looked like a good person. But he looked past you, maybe he looked through you as if you weren't there. As he passed, he splatted through a puddle, which started a continent leaking up from the bottoms of your trousers.

Maybe this description isn't even close to your own lonely, because your lonely's made of crowds. Maybe instead, musk-and-sweat-smelling bodies are compressing you on every side, as you're being pushed toward a wall in front of the bandstand. Those strangers' shirts are bleeding into yours, and their greasy hair is getting dreadlocked with your own. You feel yourself crumpling like foil, and you can't raise your arms, and even if you could scream, no one would hear you above the throbbing of the drums. And you've never been so alone.

Here's the point. When you're in a highly sensitized state of emotion, giving that emotion a name may make you feel better, but it won't help even your friends share your experience. That's because "love" and "angry" and "lonely" are inherently limp, like clothes that have been through the washing machine a few too many times. If you hold them up to the light, you'll see they've gone patchily transparent. So put them in the Goodwill pile and don't look back. You won't be bereft at all. Instead, you'll find what was hanging out of sight behind the ones you wore every day—spangly dresses maybe, and turquoise coats. Who knows what strange shoes? So get out there and look. Look in *your* closet. Because what I haven't said yet is that you can get away with writing about love or any other emotion and still be completely fresh, as long as you're using details only you know.

You see, detail is the scrip of poetry. In other words, it's critical, especially when you're starting, to stay absolutely away from naming an emotion. Instead, show your reader what you mean. It's your choice of particulars out of the whole starry sky that will define you in your work. In short, one of your main tasks as a writer is to find the "you" in what is not you.

But What if the Reader Doesn't "Get it"?

I covered this point before when I was talking about editing, but it's worth bringing up again, because it's crucial. With some practice, you'll start coming up with telling, idiosyncratic details and have the confidence to leave them in. Still, even when you succeed at "showing," you'll find yourself tempted also to "tell." Because you'll want people to know that, even though what they're reading may look simple, it's not. Giving in to this impulse is like lumbering your poems with price tags, the cumbersome ones that set off alarms if you try to leave the store. When you think about it, you can see how tacky you'd look with price tags dangling off your hat, your sweater, your pants. You'd trip over them if you left them on your shoes. Right? Of course you're right.

WHAT IF TEACHERS DON'T "GET IT"?

Vis à vis interpretation of poems...I've had several knock-down drag-out discussions with English teachers over the years (first mine, then my children's) because they insisted that a certain poem needed to be interpreted this way or that and rejected alternative approaches, however well-reasoned.

As a kid, I wondered why they were so closed-minded. Wasn't it good rather than bad if I figured things out for myself? But as an adult, I think I know the answer. The fact that there's no easy packaged answer to "What does this mean?" doesn't bother the right-brained, but like everyone else, not all English teachers have functioning right brains. What happens to the ones who don't is that over time they become more and more convinced that any recalcitrant poem must be in some code—which is a problem from their point of view, because if they don't "get it" themselves, how can they teach it? So they read what other people have had to say, with special attention to what the poet's said, and *Voilà!,* now they know the answer. In other words, second-hand reading works like Rolaids for certain purveyors of English—now that they know they know what they want on the test, they can stop fretting and go get some coffee in the teacher's lounge.

HOW POEMS AREN'T ESSAYS

One thing I know for sure. If I'd wanted to make a point, I'd have written an essay. If I write a poem, I'm doing it because there's something I know I can't get to any other way than by casting a line over waters I can't see into. I've caught some very odd fish like this, some with rainbows on their sides, some so ugly I can't imagine them feeding on anything but mud, and over the years many that I couldn't find, thumbing through my book of fish.

Furthermore, when I've finished a poem, I can never fit it neatly into one package. It bleeds through, the paper is cut too small, the tape softens, the string breaks. But this doesn't bother me, because I know that when I'm reading other people's poetry, it's not the intellectual cleverness of it all that wins me over. For me, the *sine qua non* of any poem is "Does it make me feel something?" Then, if it passes that gate, the next question is "Does what I'm feeling make any difference?" I don't claim to be objective in any of this. Neither poetry nor its impact is objective. You may be so thrilled you'll need smelling salts when you read the Language poets. The fact that I don't doesn't mean that they aren't any good. It just means that when I read Language poetry, the top of my head stays firmly on, which tells me that Language poetry's not for me and I need to look elsewhere.

BEYOND THE PRIMARY COLORS

When I find a poem I love, I get something like a galvanic skin response. That I can't name what I'm feeling, that my feeling probably doesn't have a name, doesn't bother me, because, from years of touching and being touched in this way, I've gotten past the primary emotional colors.

In this respect, I think poetry has a lot in common with painting. A beginning painter starts out like a child singing the rainbow song— red and orange, green and blue, shining yellow, and maybe, if she's really exceptional, heliotrope instead of purple too. She doesn't realize at first how many colors there are and how many variations on each there can be, and she has no idea in the beginning that simply putting one shade of green next to another can change both shades completely. As she gets accustomed to the feel of the brush in the valley between her first finger and thumb, as she studies over the years the dividing rivers on her palette, and if, after all this, she's lucky, then she'll begin to get the power of the spectrum spread out before her, quivering on the floor.

Let's take a simpler example: black-and-white photography. When you first start looking at photographs, you notice black, white, and maybe one or two shades of grey. But how poor your eyes are, beginning looker, and what a treat you have coming. There are hundreds, even thousands, of shades of grey. In other words, as a poet what you're fishing for isn't just the nameable emotions but also the more complicated ones. Finding them in yourself, pulling them up dripping red river water, can keep you happy for the rest of your life. Believe me, I know.

REPRISE: LET YOUR READER HAVE THE POEM

If, after all I've told you, you're still tempted to spell things out, don't do it. Trust me. No one likes being preached to. Remember how annoying that prissy little girl in your fifth grade class was, the one with the matching hair ribbons and the perpetual hand in the air, the one who sighed loudly if the teacher didn't call on her, the one who always had to be right no matter what?

Besides, when you've been at this for a few years, you'll find that if you say what you came to say, in words that belong to you, most of your readers will get what you meant them to get. And if they don't happen to get "it," but they liked the poem anyhow, hooray for you. Look how your poem has a life. Look what you put into it without even knowing.

ON PERSISTENCE

"Okay okay," you say. I've heard the sermon. I believe you. But how do I do that? Because most of the time, when I sit down to write, nothing comes out but clichés, and I end up wanting to tear everything I've done into little tiny pieces and flush it down the toilet. Well, here's the truth. What you're telling me is that you're normal. No matter how long you write, you're going to be producing garbage some high percentage of the time. I still do, after thirty years, and so, they say, do all my friends. If you aren't willing to write badly, the fact is that you'll never learn to write well. This holds for other fields than poetry, too. I used to tell my programming students not to worry if they programmed stupidly at first, because the definition of learning is making mistakes. No mistakes, no growth. If you write badly long enough, sooner or later something will take you over and you'll find, to your surprise, that you're writing really well.

Here's an example from another area. I used to run lots of road races. Since my favorite distance was 15K, almost always at some point my body would tell me in no uncertain terms, "You can't do this, you're going to have to stop." And yet, I knew I wouldn't stop no matter how much that slow-down voice buzzed in my ear. How could I be sure? Experience. I knew I wouldn't stop, because in all the races I'd run, I'd never stopped. And when I'm between poetry rushes, I still feel exactly the way I used to feel in the middle of a race. You're not getting anywhere, says the voice. Face facts. You've written your last good poem. You'll never get past this rubbish. But so far I always have, and, so far, on the other side there's always been something new.

HOW TO TROLL FOR DETAILS

Okay, good you've bought into this too. You're willing to keep going. Let's talk about how, practically speaking, you can get at the right details for you. One way to start is to look behind your failed poem. If you take the central idea and cluster it, physical things may jump at you from the edges of the paper so that you can delete the center and, essentially, use those edges. Another is to translate your poem into some other language. I don't mean that literally (though a free translation program like Babblefish can yield some interesting results if you take it into another language then back to English) nor do I mean using mock-translation (as in chapter 1). What I mean instead is this. Let's say you're writing about a failed marriage. Here are some examples of languages: the dialect of the room you lived in with that person; the syntax of your neck and left shoulder right now; the brat-speech of your car—its ratty seat covers, its gearshift, its battery, its passenger side door, the pieces of its engine; the language of dinner—the kitchen, the meal—describe the food steaming on the counter waiting to be carried, the dining room. And so on.

ALL THE TIME

If you've been living the way we've been talking about in this book, you won't have to start from ground zero every time you need a metaphor. If you didn't hear me last time, let me tell you again. You're going to have a very stony row to hoe if you're a poet only when you sit down. So if you aren't doing this already, you want to get into the habit of asking every event and object around you, "What are you like?" Okay. "What else are you like?" and then when you get home, writing down as many answers to those questions as you can find.

Keep in mind you have other sources of metaphoric ammunition available besides what's around you right now. By the time we've lived a while, almost all of us will have been exposed to some skill whose mastery will have required learning a new set of words. When I was little, all the girls in my convent school had to learn embroidery. So I have in my repertoire "big-eyed needles," multi-stranded threads with colors that shade into one another, "cross- and daisy- stitches." Maybe you took ballet. If you'll think back, your teacher didn't tell you, "Get up on your tiptoes," or, "Spread your feet out," or, "Bend down." She said something like *"plié"* or *"relevee"* instead, because she wanted to say not generally but exactly, how to move next. Or maybe you've studied cabinet-making, so you know what "dado" and "rabbet" and "milling" mean, and you can tell us the strengths and weaknesses of woods like pine, which is soft, birch which is refined, and poplar, which seldom finishes to one color. Is a metaphor beginning to stir here? Maybe you live with tools like clamps, routers, pocket cutters, chisels, and bandsaws. Not everyday words, are they? Or maybe you sail— sailing has its own, gorgeously metaphoric vocabulary: "main," "jib," "spinnaker," "genoa," "mainsail," "storm sail," and its own language, starting with "Hard alee!" before you come about so your company isn't knocked out by the boom swinging over.

USE YOUR EXPERTISE

I've worked in high schools and middle schools and often I've had students who started out uninterested in, even hostile, to writing. Once, I remember, it was a high-school football player, an African-American boy, who made it clear from the first day that he wasn't about to do this stuff. That didn't bother me, because I'd seen lack of interest turn to excitement once a student realized how much he/she could accomplish. But it did have to be dealt with from the beginning, so once I'd gotten the other students working on the first assignment, I went over to his desk and said, "Look. You know more about football than anyone else in this room, so I'd like for you to write about football. And don't worry, it won't matter what the assignment is, because if you work football right, it can take in everything else." I followed that up with a few amateurish examples since I don't know much about football—he was the expert—and left him to his own devices. He did really, really well. I'm not saying he was a born poet, but he did find some things in himself I don't think he knew were there. And he made me proud, because on my last day, he pushed through all the other students to shake my hand. Such was the power of his metaphor.

So, look around. Somewhere you'll have some treasure trove like this. It won't matter if it was recent, because, as Kenneth Koch once said, "You're all the ages you ever were," so if at any point you owned it, you won't have forgotten. If it was a long time ago, sit down and list every term you can dredge up from that experience. In fact, even if it wasn't a long time ago, it's not a bad idea to write down everything you can remember about the subject. You know how hard it is to come up with a word or a movie title or someone's name on demand, even when it's right on the tip of your tongue.

Besides, if you already have a list, you can look at it when you're under pressure. Don't have anything in mind when you make the list. Just outfit it as extensively as you can, and put it someplace you can find it. You won't use this stuff in every poem, of course, but there will be times you will. When you do, what you write will be grounded, because you'll be writing in a specialized arena most of us, when we read your poems, will wish we also had access to.

ON DETAIL THAT'S NOT LIKE WHAT IT REFERS TO

One last thing I want to tell you about detail. When you're choosing among metaphors, remember the most exciting metaphors are often the ones in which the things being compared are least obviously related. I read an article in *The New York Times* once that said of music something like, "The moment of greatest dimension is always the moment of greatest tension." I think that's true of poetry, too. So when you're casting around for that simile or metaphor, take the wildest chances you can. Chances like going through rapids. Chances like picking up tropical animals that might be poisonous. This is the part where you don't censor. Spill everything you can possibly think of and don't pause to object. When you look at what you've done, sure you'll often decide that what you've written doesn't apply. But when it does... "Wow!" you'll say. "Wow! Wow! Wow! A polar bear really is like a buttercup!" You'll be excited, not only because you know what you've just said is true, but also because you know that no one could have thought of it but you.

YOU CAN DO THIS!

Okay now, here you are. You've been casting around for a year or two, maybe longer, and you know, because you read a lot, that what you're coming up with isn't all that great. So you're creeping toward discouragement and beginning to wonder if writing poetry is for you after all. I've overheard famous poets tell people like you that you might as well stop writing, the implication being that the sooner for the literary world the better. Once, years ago, it was a girl sobbing in front of an elevator out of which the famous poet's dismissive voice was issuing like a god's. "Why should you want to write?" it was saying.

"You have no talent. Give it up." And the door closed, and he went down. I knew that poet rather well at the time, but I never forgave him for that moment.

Not only is it rude and insensitive to treat anyone this way, it's also wrong-headed, because categorical dismissals like the one I've just described make an assumption that isn't accurate—that fluency, if you weren't born with it, can't be acquired. The difference between someone who develops into a fine writer and someone who doesn't is never simply talent. As much as talent, the difference is persistence. What causes people to persist, I think, is nearly always passion, which is also what in the end will lend their words depth and edge.

When I started writing, my poems were pretty terrible, and I can easily imagine this poet telling me exactly what he told that young woman. And if he had, I'd have curled up and gone away, because I had no defenses then and, since he seemed to be in a position of authority, I would have believed him. But don't you make that mistake. If anyone ever talks to you that way, directly or by implication, ignore them. Say, "Oh yeah? Come back in a few years. Then you'll see." Because if you really want to do this, and if you care enough not to give up, the truth is that you can.

EXERCISES
Panning for Gold

1. Writing about traumatic events is good therapy. Often that sort of "spill" was never intended as anything but, and that's fine. But if you want your work to last past the occasion that sparked it, here's something to try. Put the incident in the center of a piece of paper and draw a circle around it. Now, cluster outwards every word you can think of that relates to the five senses as experienced in that incident: smell (acrid, smoky, chemical, exhaust, citrus) touch, (rough, freckled, bumpy, slick), taste (sweet, bitter, tangy, metallic), sight (black, red, lilac), sound (scream, sob, twitter). Circle each of those and draw lines connecting them to the center. If other words occur to you, put those down, too. Now, from each of those words, cluster outwards. Be as physical as you can. Don't think about the event at the center, only the words. Rhyme them, free-associate them, don't read what you're doing. Do this until you have a full page of this. Then, try to connect things at the edges of opposite sides of the page. You'll find they relate in surprising ways, both to each other and back to the center. Write something using those. You may want to put some facts in before you're through, but don't do that now.

2. Use the same clustering technique to write a poem or a start at a poem about one of the big emotions—love, hate, jealousy, and so on. Here's a poem of mine that could have begun like that.

Love

She tries it on, like a dress.
She decides it doesn't fit
and starts to take it off.
Her skin comes, too.

3. For the idea of this one, I'm in debt to my friend Jon Rybicki. Think of someone in your life with whom you have a big unresolved issue. Think how a little kid will take an adult's chin in his hand and turn it so the adult has to look at him. Now, what you're going to write is what goes on from this sentence—to that person: *This is what I want you to see.* Don't be abstract, get physical.

4. Read through a sheaf of your or someone else's poems. Underline every vague noun or adjective. See what you feel you can live without. It won't be all of it. Then, take one of the poems and substitute a physical word for each of the abstractions you have left.

5. Make a list of some members of your family. Now, under each name, write some objects that come to mind. See how completely you can get at the person using those objects. Don't limit yourself to items that person would choose, like your Dad's favorite pipe. Think about what "means" them to *you.* Here are some examples: for a teenage son, sweaty socks, because he leaves a trail of them in your house; for your sister, dirty blue sheets, because she doesn't change them, also because they're a metaphor for her life; tangerine blossoms for your cousin, because they grow in her yard and because she's innocent like that. And so on.

6. Write as steamy a sexual fantasy as you can. Now, make a list of every part of a car you can think of and replace each noun in your poem with either a car part or a kitchen utensil.

CHAPTER
8
MASKS

"Man is least himself when he speaks in his own person.
Give him a mask and he will tell you the truth."
—Oscar Wilde

Though this is clearly a statement in which Wilde is in full pose mode, I think there's something to what he says. I also think that masks offer more than the all-about-me rewards he implies, and in this chapter I'm going to tell you why you should at least try them. But this suggestion comes with a warning: unless you do it for the right reasons, you risk your personas coming off phony. When I edited a magazine, I used to suspect some people of writing persona poetry not because they were driven from inside to do that, but because they thought that using a non me voice would make them stand out because of its (apparent) modesty. The problem was that it wouldn't have worked, because an astute editor, tapping on that tree trunk, would have heard it was hollow and turned them down.

PROLOGUE: WHAT HISTORY IS

Now that I have the wrong reason out of the way, I'd like to tell you a story. Bear with me. By the time you get to the end, you'll see why it's relevant. One fall back in the 1970s, I was teaching a large class called "Computers in Modern Society" and was halfway through a sentence about how John Vincent Atanasoff invented the electronic digital computer when another November crossed my mind. I was about to mention it when I had an epiphany. This is what it was: I suddenly realized that not one of my 200 students, some assiduously taking notes, others even more assiduously reading *The Alligator*, had been born that day.

I remember walking numbly around the Stanford campus after the suspense was over and Kennedy was gone. And I remember how my numbness turned to anger as I passed two guys strolling by, laughing together at some joke. I wanted to grab them by their smug madras shirts and hiss: "How can you? Don't you know the President is dead?" I didn't do it, of course; I was much too shy back then, but that was what I was feeling, and in no uncertain terms.

After the assassination, which had been preceded by the Cuban missile crisis, when we used to wake up listening for bombs, I don't think my generation ever felt truly safe again. Without ever thinking it through, I'd assumed that the events of that November afternoon had marked not only us but would also mark every generation that followed. But looking into the dark of that auditorium on that other November day, it hit me, as if it had been one of those bombs, how wrong I'd been.

Until then I'd conceptualized history as an interaction between energies, analogous to the movement of geologic plates. But now I saw, not intellectually but via a chill that ran all the way to my toes, how specific it really was. I also understood that the history of those years was going to consist of my memories of events like the Kennedy assassination, and the other Kennedy assassination, the King assassination, and the war in Vietnam. As your memories do, if you're old enough. In other words, I finally got what I should have understood years before—that the reason assassinations and wars and displacements are so important is that they changed forever the lives of millions of people, and that signifying events are specific to their time—the assassinations and the Cuban missile crisis to my generation, World War II to my parents', the Depression that preceded it to their parents', and probably the Challenger disaster to these students, who'd have run out of their classrooms to look up at the blue air through which a two-headed caterpillar was slowly falling.

Understanding that history consists of one pair of eyes at a time was the first step in my journey toward masks. The second, clinching step had to do with my own geographical background. Before I moved to Gainesville, I'd lived in obviously spectacular places—Northern California, Greece, Mexico. But here in north-central Florida, it was clear that if I were ever going to belong, and I did passionately want to, I was going to have to pay attention. So I studied plants, birds, and trees. I canoed some clear waters and some red ones. I found my heart in salt marshes.

But the day of the Atanasoff class, I realized that natural history wasn't going to be enough, because it was horizontal—it stopped with the first inch of soil. I knew nothing of the vertical. In other words, I was ignorant of the stories that had happened under my feet. And here, where the tail of my fur stole met the teeth, I knew what I had to do. I went to the Florida history section of the library.

LIVING HISTORY

I started with secondary sources, for their context. But those didn't taste exactly natural, rather like sodas, and the more of them I drank, the thirstier I got. When I got thirsty enough, the librarians obliged, bringing me brimming boxes whose envelopes threatened to crumble as I laid bare the letters they held. What a voyeur I felt, holding these messages in my hands. How could the woman writing a husband away at the Civil War have imagined that a hundred years later a stranger would be reading this? How could she have imagined that the words that hadn't moved a stroke since she set them down weren't going to stay safe in the privacy of their envelope?

I wasn't reading the letters and journals with a thief's eyes. I just wanted to see what it had been like to live in Florida a hundred-and-fifty, even two-hundred, years ago. But after reading the letters that arrived at my table smelling-of-yellowed-paper, it became clear that nothing I read had what I was looking for, because their writers' lives weren't lived in the lines but between them. Whether this was because the relatives who'd donated the materials had censored something or because men and women in those days just didn't write intimately, I don't know. One night I dreamed the real stories had been told in lemon juice, and I saw them, emerging warm and brown under my hot iron. But when I woke up, they vanished.

What I'm trying to say here is that my visits to the library left me in some curious way without knowledge. The letter writers and I had eaten different breakfasts. We hadn't known each other's quiet moments, the still times being for women like me the important ones. What I was feeling, I think, was the difference between driving to the top of a mountain and hiking up the back side. It's the same view, but you own it or you don't.

Most of the letters that spoke to me were written by women—to get closer to them, I decided that the only way to understand these women would be to be one. I started with paraphrasing letters written by a

Civil War wife named Octavia Stephens and caulked the factual gaps from secondary sources. But no matter how hard I worked trying to get her right, I could tell Octavia wasn't home, and finally I abandoned the effort. Then one afternoon six months later, when I was working on something else, Jane began emerging under my fingers. Though I'd never seen Jane's letters—I couldn't have, she's fiction—she was clearly of Octavia's world. I sensed that if I listened carefully enough, she would tell me what to do, and in the course of the next few months, she did.

On Multiple Lives

When Jane fell silent, Julia and Patsy followed in her wake. By this time I'd viscerally realized something else that had been only intellectually obvious to me before—that this "I," this Lola whose book you're reading, is just an accident of time and place. This idea must have cracked something open in me, because after that all sorts of other voices started coming and I wrote them down as they arced, silver or red or gold as the case might have been; then, knowing they wouldn't be back, I let them go.

Through these others, I was an unfaithful wife in Greenland in the year 1000. I was a bird-loving boy in Argentina in the 1880s. I was (reluctantly) Columbus. I was a young homesteader in Pennsylvania in the days when passenger pigeons darkened the air so thickly they could be knocked down with sticks. I was Mary Peake of Ilkley, who, pregnant with her first child, fell from her horse and died. I was an English painter living in Mexico in the 1970s. I was the Florida farm wife who lives across the pasture from me.

I stuck with personas for several years, because I was fascinated with the new world each one opened for me. But one day, the source of the uncomfortable feeling that had been creeping up on my arm for months identified itself: this is getting easy. I knew then that I had to try something else. It's not a good thing to be addicted, not to anything, except maybe poetry itself.

I hope, listening to my story, you'll have been feeling some stirrings inside yourself. I'm sure you remember that when you were little (unless you were one of those rare kids who's always known he/she wanted to be a doctor) you tried all kinds of futures on for size. Personally, I wanted to be a ballerina. It didn't matter that I couldn't even touch my toes. I also wanted to be, serially and sometimes simultaneously, a painter, a pianist, Dale Evans, and an explorer. Oh, and Sheena Queen of the Jungle, because she wore leopard skins and what my mother said was a tasteless bracelet on her left ankle, which made me like it all the more. But with the years those potentials dropped away until I was left with only one life. And yet, not.

You get the point. By trying other people on for size, you can transcend every one of your physical/temporal limitations. You can change your sex, you can live in the past or future. It doesn't matter that you happen to be quadriplegic. You can climb a mountain. Of course, you can get some of the effect by reading first person writings set in those voices, those times. But, believe me, that won't be the same as having lived with those people the way you will have if you've written them.

RESEARCH: WHAT'S LEFT OUT IS POWERFUL

When you do decide to take on someone else's identity, real or otherwise, it's important not to rush out and start writing. Spend a lot of listening time first. Talk to the person if he or she is still alive. Read around in his/her era if not, and keep in mind that you always have the choice of using a real person or inventing one. As you go, be sure to write down every fact that strikes you as interesting, whether it seems relevant at the time or not. Then, when you've exhausted all the books and primary sources you can find, write down your everyday questions, like, "What did she wear on her feet? What kinds of vegetables would she have grown?" Once you've accumulated a good list of those, track down someone who knows the answers. If you can, get your expert talking. People like that always know a lot you don't, and you may well hear something that will sing for you once you do start writing.

Let me stress something I implied a minute ago. As you do this kind of research, you always want to accumulate more knowledge than you'll directly use, because when you finish your piece, all the facts you didn't put in will be backing up the ones you did. I'm convinced that if you don't know more than you're telling, you'll end up with a façade, and that won't work, because truth takes a whole house, the bedrooms you never go into, the baths you don't mention.

By the way, if you never write a single line of poetry after you do your research, think what you'll have gained. Without leaving home, you'll have enjoyed some productive time somewhere else. People and places will be real to you, which were never real before. And whether you go into them or not, your head will be outfitted with new rooms, full of exotic knick-knacks. You will, in other words, be that much more alive.

Most of the time, of course, you will end up writing at least some poems in the afterglow of your research, if for no other reason than because you've been going around in the 18th century for weeks and the only way to get back to the 20th is to spill the 18th, like pouring the bucket of water you've been carrying, back into the sea. Or you've been living as a single mother in a homeless shelter for months, and it's time to shut the door on her life and go back to your own. Same bucket, different water.

EVEN EVIL MASKS ARE YOU

Now, let's carry the bucket back up the hill to the quote from Wilde with which I started this chapter. I'll suggest to you now that the reason you choose one individual's voice over another's has to be that, at least on some level, you identify with him/her. "How could anyone identify with certain people?" I can hear you say, especially if you're thinking of a certain famous sequence in Hitler's voice. I see what you mean, but wait a minute. Evil is one component of human (as opposed to animal) nature. If we don't know what evil looks like, in other people and by extension in ourselves, how can we know to fight it when it walks in the door?

The problem, of course, is that even if we grant that for reasons of self-protection we should look evil in the face, it's nevertheless threatening to explore it using our own voices. We're afraid, and naturally so, that someone might think we'd really put a razor blade in that little Batman's Halloween apple.

That's where masks come in. By becoming players with our faces hidden, we can explore aspects of human nature that we wouldn't normally feel comfortable talking about—the policeman who assaults an arrestee with a plunger in a station restroom, for instance, the incestuous father who leaves his daughter afraid to go to sleep, the eighth grader who takes an arsenal to school. Once we've looked at the world through those alter-eyes, we're more likely to be honest when we return to ourselves.

BOTTOM LINE: MASKS CAN EXPRESS YOUR COMPLEXITY

Of course most of our personas won't be evil; they'll just be people with lives that happen not to be ours. And, good, bad or in-between, if we let those personas live as more than puppets, sooner or later they'll do things we weren't expecting. One day, you'll look at the lines that have just come from your fingers, and you'll get a chill. "Oh, my God," you'll say to yourself, "that's me."

Castings, which was my second book of Florida women, taught me much more about myself than I'd learned from my first, which, aside from a couple of monologues, was deeply self-involved. Jane taught me a courage I didn't possess and which, if I'd not been writing in her voice, I'd never have known existed. From Julia, I who know nothing about commerce, learned about the kind of selling that turns hair white, as if it had just seen something terrible. And from Patsy, my opaque lady, I learned the cunning of power and the power of cunning. These women enriched my life in my own century more than I can say, and even now, Jane comes with me when I fly.

But in *Castings,* and for many years afterwards, I avoided the hard issues both in my own voice and in the personas I chose. My characters for the most part came out winners and so by implication did I. When they didn't, I could always say, "Well, of course, this is fiction." It wasn't until I reached my late forties that I risked not looking good in print. In other words, two steps have marked my growth as a writer—the mask and the dropping of the mask. As I've gotten older, I've come to believe, at least for myself, that as long as I'm not willing to come off imperfect in my writing, I'm not fully representing who I am. Maybe I don't have to do that. But more and more I'm convinced that truth requires I do, because a flat person isn't a whole person.

I think this will happen to you, too. When you've been walking around in other people's lives, you'll start seeing your own through their eyes, the sort of stories that come out at dinner or when you're sitting in the pasture watching the pond and a crow flaps by that reminds you of something Jane read this morning. And after that, when you go back to your own voice, as you're bound to sooner or later, you'll find you won't be the same "I". Your new "I" will catch the light differently when you walk around it, and as you open the door and walk in, conversation will stop, and strangers, beautiful, dangerous, or both, will look up and smile.

EXERCISES
Not You

1. Write a monologue in the voice of a villain from a fairy tale.

2. Write a poem about you in your mother's/father's voice.

3. Write a poem in the voice of the person you dislike the most.

4. Find a newspaper article that profiles someone and write a monologue using that person's voice. Be sure to mimic the person's syntax.

5. Write a poem from the point of view of someone of the opposite sex/sexual orientation than you. Do this first as someone in a different part of the life cycle from you, then as someone who's your contemporary.

6. Think of a place and time in history that interest you. Do a library search using that period and that place. Pick two or three source books that look primary. Go to the library stacks and choose some books from that area. Use primary sources, such as diaries and contemporary accounts, at least half of them not the ones you went to find. Now, read through all of them and write down anything that stimulates your imagination. Make up a person to suit the time and setting and, starting from those details and using the first person, tell the story of something that happened to him/her. The incident doesn't need to be earth-shaking.

7. Write a poem from the point of view of an animal.

8. Write a poem from the point of view of a machine.

9. Write a poem in the voice of someone living one-hundred years in the future. Don't forget to consider how language may have changed by then.

CHAPTER

9

ELEPHANTS

If you persist in poetry long enough, sooner or later you'll find yourself at some point along a style continuum at one extreme of which is the poet who writes essentially the same poem over and over, and at the other the poet who changes modes so often that he/she risks not perfecting any of them. As long as you avoid the extremes, at least in the way I've presented them—and I'll correct those descriptions in a minute—I don't think any position you may take is misguided.

Do you remember the story of the blind men and the elephant? There are three blind men, and an elephant. Since each of the men is positioned at a different point along the elephant's body, each has a different definition of "elephant". The first blind man says that an elephant is like an air hose, but hairy. The second says that no, an elephant is a rope with a tassel at the end. The third says the first two are all wrong. An elephant is really a mountain in drought, a vast living area of cracked earth on which nothing can survive.

Now as far as they go, each of these definitions is correct. Yet none of these men has seen the elephant, nor will any of them ever see it, the premise being that the men are blind. Still, even in the story, it isn't blindness that's a metaphor for limitation—because each blind man could have moved to a new spot, and by moving, added to his definition of what an elephant is. The fact that he didn't, that was his limitation.

THE STYLE CONTINUUM

If we think of the elephant as the animal of life possibilities, we have choices. At one extreme, we can focus forever on whatever part of the elephant we happen to encounter first; at the other, we can run wildly from one end of the beast to the other, with the risk that the running itself may become our lives. Or, if we are Aristotelians, we can choose any number of stances in the middle.

We might imagine the elephant as counterpoint, with each part having its own melody line. In this case, a composer might limit herself to the soprano part. Or a woodworker limit himself (is it really limitation?) to cypress extracted from the bottoms of rivers, from which he fashions small boxes whose openings are concealed until someone is patient enough to find with his fingers the nearly invisible slits where the wood hesitates. Some poets, Billy Collins, for example, have made this kind of choice. I don't mean that his emotional concerns haven't changed over time, but I do mean that you can tell a Collins poem from across the room because it's always in the same modality.

The time-honored philosophical rationale for the one-path choice—Tennyson expressed it in "Flower in a Crannied Wall"—is that since each part of the universe contains the whole, the best way to understand it is to focus on a single element. Vuillard did that with paint—by spending his entire art in one small house, picturing his mother and his sister against ever-more-complexly patterned backgrounds.

I think the most successful example of the other extreme—trying out every melody line in an effort to sing the whole elephant—is another painter, Picasso, whose different periods a naive observer would never identify as coming from the same hand. If you don't believe that, try comparing a blue-period piece, for instance to "Guernica" or "Girl Before a Mirror." Of course, Picasso succeeded in his choice because he had the wisdom to move on to his next phase only when he was satisfied he'd accomplished all he could with the one he was leaving. At any rate, most of us fall neither with him nor with Vuillard but somewhere in the middle.

THE PROS AND CONS OF EXTREMES

I don't think any thinking person would argue that stylistic consistency is inherently positive or negative. It seems obvious that the choice a poet makes in this regard seems to be mainly a matter of temperament. Some people feel more comfortable in one carefully crafted space. Others, on the other hand, would be as restless there as if they've just been told they have to live the rest of their lives in a very small boat.

It's also obvious, I think, that in the way medicines can have side effects, each extreme has its pitfalls. Sometimes, for instance, I get claustrophobic when I read a certain poet who, I think, is relentlessly married to his approach. I can feel his hands drawn in, tense with suppressed energy. I get the sense that what he'd want, if only he weren't so repressed, would be to punch out the sides of the box. Other writers, though their range is just as confined, feel gem-like to me, as naturally and wisely compressed as diamonds. I've put in some considerable time working out why I respond positively to some of these poets and not to others, because I thought understanding that would help me know when, in my own case, it was time to move on. In the next section, I'll explain what I learned.

HOW TO TELL WHEN TO GO

Let's take as a test case a photographer who has fallen in love with ants and as a consequence spends his/her life pointing a camera at little tiny insects milling in and out of holes. That's certainly specialized enough for anyone. Is this person stuck in a box or is he/she a jeweler? I think the answer to this question may come down to a pair of other questions. First, has he succeeded in producing useful and exciting close-ups of ants? Let's assume he has. Will he go on succeeding? Well, the answer to that depends on what he does if, at some point, he stales.

There are, I think, two sub-considerations to this second question, and these apply to us as writers as much as to our wandering and probably itchy photographer. The first is whether this person's initial choice of focus was made out of fire. If he's succeeded so far, it probably was. The second has to do with how he reacts when and if the fire loses its momentum. Does he admit it and try to kindle another? Or does he, on the other hand, persist by the embers of the old fire, his hands still out for the warmth he remembers was there?

It's safest to stay home. If you go outside, someone might challenge you; you might get run over by a car. This kind of fear can cripple people so completely that they become unable to leave the house, and if someone didn't go to the supermarket for them, these people would, literally, starve. For poets, too, it's a real temptation not to leave the territory whose rules we know. And yet staying home too long can mean death, a lingering, if writerly, tubercular death.

SWITCHING: A CASE HISTORY

I know this from experience. As I told you earlier in our conversation, in a slightly different context, I started writing first-person fictions in the early seventies. Eventually I got to the point where I knew that certain magazines would pretty reliably publish them, and that all I had to do was keep producing. But more and more I felt trapped. Persona poetry had gotten relatively easy (not easy, nothing's easy) for me; it was sounding fine; it was even up to a certain level of craft. And yet, everyone whose voice I was writing in those days, whoever the ostensible speaker was, began to sound uncomfortably like everyone else. It took me a while to admit that to myself, but when I finally did, I knew I had to stop it right there. I had to go back to the really blank page.

That made me really nervous. I'd stayed with persona poems so long I wasn't at all sure I hadn't run myself right out of imaginative resources. Also, I was worried that if I did take another approach, even successfully, I'd lose my audience. Still, I did what I had to do, and let go. At first I was completely lost. I cast around unsuccessfully for a while, quite a while. Finally, I began writing lyrics about playing the piano. I was passionate about that—still am. The only trouble was that I'd been right to worry about whether the magazines that had supported me before would stand by me now. Though they tended to sign my rejection slips as a nod to my ex-status, the slips still said "No." And it wasn't just one of my old venues that started turning me down—it was all of them. For a long time, no one else seemed to like what I was doing, either.

I think I know what happened. The places I'd been publishing had invited me to dinner as a woman and suddenly I'd showed up as a man. It was also, I think, that they might have seen the new poems as abstract; they definitely weren't daily in the way the history poems had been.

I wasn't tempted to go back, though, because the music poems felt like a stretch. I knew even then how important keeping loose can be. It can even, if indirectly, save your life. In that context, it's interesting that most heart attacks happen in the morning, when someone gets up too fast from bed, without stretching first.

As it turned out, the change eventually paid off. *Forty-Four Ambitions,* the book that came out of those poems, has been lucky. It was reviewed in music magazines; it's even been used as a text in some music schools. But *Ambitions* wasn't the end of my lyrics about music. I was still hooked and still writing. Finally, I accumulated enough poems for a sequel; but when I looked at putting one together, it was obvious that the accumulation was a losing proposition. About that time, exactly when I needed it, I heard a speaker, quoting someone else (unfortunately, I haven't been able to track the source), say, "Throw out merely good."

Okay, okay, I said. I heaved a big sigh, and I started over. I threw a lot of paint at a lot of what turned out to be many highly disposable canvases. Finally, I started writing about my roots in Mexico, in a completely different tone from the music poems, and exactly the same thing happened.

The devotees of the music poems didn't like the Mexican poems. To find homes for those, I had to look for new magazines. One of those that did seem to like the Mexican stuff, which eventually solidified into *Extranjera*, was *The Missouri Review*. A few years later, I thought I'd send them some of what I'd thought were my best leftover music poems. Of course, they turned them down.

I'm sorry to go on about myself. I'm only doing it because I'm the only case I know well enough to use to show you what may happen if you decided to experience as much of the elephant as possible. By the way, I'm well aware that I'm almost surely exploring any one elephant part less perfectly than someone who spends a life there. But moving around suits me because my poetic knack is, I think, sneak thievery.

No matter what, I know I'm no good at slow pans. Another reason, and maybe the main one, that I keep moving is that it's my way of taking a chance, and, as you'll see in the next chapter, that's important to me.

A Word for the Other Way

None of this is to say that a poet who sticks with one part of the elephant isn't risking. Suppose she decides on the tail. Over time she risks trading all the rough and lovely freshness that struck her when she started, in favor of a mannered, essentially blasé, beauty. And yet, if she can succeed the rewards are huge, because putting the tenth coat of varnish on a piece of wood, the one only the maker will know is there, is a satisfaction beyond what most of us will ever experience.

In other words, I really do think that, as I just said, this comes down to personality. Because I lack the requisite patience for that tenth coat, I rationalize that not moving on would be giving in. I do have one consolation, though. I'll never exhaust the elephant, not even if I get to every part of its body, because by the time I show up at the other end again, I'll have forgotten I ever saw it. It's like what happens with the Golden Gate Bridge. The minute they finish one end, it's time to start painting from the other. Besides, I'll never get the whole elephant clear in my mind, because it's too big an animal for me, or anyone else, to see. Meanwhile, what I'm doing frightens me. It looks like a long way down, and there's a lot of wind.

THE MAN WHO SAW THE ELEPHANT

I'm going to finish this chapter with a joke current in California during the gold rush. Its punchline is dear to me because all my life I've been driven toward something I don't have and can't name. It doesn't matter that I know that this hunger may find during my whole lifetime only a few moments of satisfaction. In fact, that may even be the point. You can see what you think about that when you've heard me out.

The story goes like this: Once upon a time there lived a farmer who had never seen an elephant. One morning, as he was picking up some chicken scratch, he heard from his friends at the feed store that a circus would be coming to town the next week, and that with that circus there would be an elephant. Now the farmer didn't have the money to go to the circus, but he became obsessed with the idea of seeing the elephant anyway. So, on the morning the circus was to arrive, he hitched up his horse, packed his wagon with eggs for market, and started out on the road. When he got to a wide place, he pulled off to the side. And he waited. He waited for hours. Finally, a rumbling line of bright-painted wagons could be seen coming through the dust. As it approached, it became obvious that there wasn't room for two wagons on that road, not even if one was pulled to the side. Still the farmer stood his ground. He wanted to see that elephant. In the end, the circus wagons barreled by, knocking his wagon into a ditch, breaking his entire load of eggs, and leaving him with a black eye, bruises, and a banged leg that would cause him to limp for the rest of his life. Yet when the wagons were past, the farmer struggled to his feet, stood in the exact middle of the road and shouted after the departing circus: "I care not a fig for all of this, for I have seen the elephant!"

Of course, the farmer hadn't really seen the elephant, any more than the blind men saw it, any more than most of the people who went to the gold rush struck gold. He only caught it out of the corner of his eye. That his glimpse cost him didn't matter—it was a price he was willing to pay. I think this elephant, at once physical and the incarnation of the universe itself, is what we poets spend our lives trying to describe. We do that in spite of our understanding that the elephant is ultimately unknowable no matter how devoted we are. And why? Because in those few instants in which we get our hands on a piece of the truth, all our hunger disappears, and we're suddenly pure joy. This is what we work for: one glimpse (and then we fall) of the elephant lumbering by.

EXERCISES
Breaking Your Mold

1. If you usually write in short lines, write a poem using extra-long ones. If you usually write in long lines, do the reverse.

2. Read a poet whose work is wildly different in approach from yours. Try to steal his/her persona by pretending you are what's called in Norse myth a shape-shifter.

3. If you usually write domestic poems, go get an issue of *Scientific American* or *Science* and write a poem using something in that issue.

4. If you usually write free verse, write ten poems, each in a different form. (You can find explanations of poetic forms on the web.)

5. If doing it would be new to you, write a poem made up entirely of dialogue.

6. If doing it would be new to you, write a poem that's a story you might tell at bedtime.

7. If doing it would be new to you, write a myth to account for something in nature—like how the sky happened to be blue, like why worms don't have legs, etc. Rudyard Kipling's *Just So Stories* could give you some ideas, or certain of A.A. Milne's poems—like one about the dormouse who lived in a bed of delphiniums (blue) and geraniums (red).

8. The following exercise is especially good if you've been writing for a few years and find yourself in a linguistic rut. Find a book of poetry or songs in a language you don't speak. Find a poem/song in the book whose first few lines have cognates (words that sound like words in English). Now "translate" the poem, by which I mean write down whatever each word sounds like to you right now. If you get stuck on a word, skip it. Don't try to make the lines consistent with each other. When you've "translated" the whole thing or most of it, go back and highlight anything that sounds interesting. Type the highlighted phrases on another sheet of paper and go on from each one, again without thinking or trying to make your "poem" coherent. After a couple of passes at this, something will start to take shape.

9. Take one page of a novel and string words together that start with the same letter as the words on the page you're looking at. An example, off my bookshelf at random, might be this, from *Twenty-Thousand Leagues Under the Sea*. "'Monsieur,' said Captain Nemo, pointing to the instruments hanging on the walls of his room. 'These are the devices needed to navigate the Nautilus.'" from which I got: "Many sad choruses, no perhaps two turbulent ibises, have opened treetops without opening rain." I typed this without thinking, so of course it doesn't make sense. On the other hand, the idea of opening treetops or rain, the idea of ibises in turbulence, those could go someplace. And that was only one sentence.

CHAPTER
10
RISKS

If you're lucky, some day you'll emerge from wherever you've been for the last several hours, and find you've written something so threatening that you want to destroy it. Right. Now. When your work makes you feel this extreme, it almost never means that the writing is awful. It means you're onto something. Put down your pickaxe for a minute and celebrate. You've struck a vein.

IT'S GOOD TO BE AFRAID

Certain of my poems scared me when I wrote them. The first time this happened, I thought my instinct to toss what I'd just written into the nearest wastebasket was my writer-self's way of telling me I'd gone too far. Now that I'm more experienced, I know that the fear I was experiencing was a good sign. That will be true in your case, too. Why? Because fear means you're risking something, and it's risk that gives your work edge. If you have any trouble seeing the benefits of edge, all you have to do is to look at it from a reader's point of view. Once you do that, you'll see that it's the sense that this matters, and dangerously, that keeps you going. It's edge that tells you you aren't reading something you already know. Because if a book's course is all that predictable, what's the point of reading it rather than some other book? Other than to pass the time, of course, or to get to sleep at night, which is where bestsellers shine. They're safe, they're relaxing, they're not confrontational. Bestsellers are, with a few exceptions, the Holiday Inns of literature. Even before you open the door, you know where the bed, the dresser, and the closet are going to be, what the bedspread will look like (flowered), and that there will be a tiny pad and pen on the nightstand.

ON ADRENALINE

But great poems are never Holiday Inns. They're those idiosyncratic hotels on side streets that bring on that apprehensive feeling you get walking into a dim lobby, the glances you and your companion exchange as you climb the stairs, the unexpected blast of wind that assaults you through warped landing windows. You know you won't know what's going to happen here until you've spent the night. What is the currency all this translates into? Adrenaline: that shock, that flash that illuminates someone's face so suddenly that you never forget it.

An adrenaline rush is good. It means you and your reader are alive. But I don't think you're going to be able to generate it unless two things happened when you were writing the poem. First, you found yourself in an unknown emotional space, and second, when that happened, you looked straight at whatever came up, often something you've been avoiding. In other words, adrenaline needs a moment in which everything around you is about to collapse. What I'm saying comes down to this. If you began and finished this poem sure of yourself, it will show. If you weren't affected by the process, then your reader won't be, either.

ON PHONY RISK

It can be tricky, though, because sometimes what looks like the unknown, what feels like fear to us at first encounter, isn't the real thing. There's a big difference between manipulation, which can feel real until you realize the whole thing is special effects, and true exploration. You can tell the difference if you pay attention, though, because special effects are odorless but risk has a smell you're bound to notice.

What I'm getting at is that I don't think the kind of risk that generates meaningful adrenaline can be reliably identified by content. In fact, sometimes I think it's easier to write about subjects like abuse, bombings, and so on than not, because they draw your reader's sympathy to such an extent that both of you are temporarily willing to forgive a certain lack of flavor. Recently, I was a finalist in a contest in Ireland in which one of the other finalists was a girl who had imagined murdering the children she didn't have. The fact that she cried as she delivered her poem did, I think, draw the sympathy of some of the audience, but the poem itself had special effects all over it, and because of that, to my mind anyhow, it wasn't deserving of reward.

Think how movies work in which children's lives are threatened. The spectators sit on the edges of their seats, and yet, when the movie's over and the lights come up, they leave the theater feeling manipulated, and by tomorrow they will have forgotten the name of the movie.

In other words, some apparently risky writing can be more attention-getting—ephemeral, than art—hopefully, lasting. Don't get me wrong. I'm well aware that there are poets who write supremely well about terrible situations: Alice Anderson, for instance, in *Human Nature*, or Carolyn Forché in *The Country Between Us*, or Sharon Olds in *Satan Says*. But for each of those, there are many writers whose poetry is therapy—as valid a reason to write as any other—but it somehow misses being more than that.

What's the difference? Well, the poem that survives the events that generated it will have encountered its writer at her deepest edge, yes, but also, in the midst of all that emotion, will have paid attention to the very personal music of language. Such a poem could easily have fallen on its face as a piece of art. But, miraculously, in all that howling wind, it listened carefully, and so it succeeded. So risk in poetry is in the truest sense about survival: to face rape, incest, war and come out as yourself and only yourself. Which means that you need to know and be able to express in exact true detail who that self is.

THE PITFALLS OF CRAFT

I've done a lot of judging over the years, and one of the factors that has made it a difficult and sometimes depressing job is how few chances I felt most of the contestants were taking. There were times when I read through piles of several hundred manuscripts and found the majority of them competently, even admirably, crafted. Yet with all that skill, the contestants felt like the talent show part of a beauty pageant. Though intellectually I knew Miss Texas was very different inside from Miss Minnesota, who was a completely different ball game from Miss Maine, I couldn't shake the sense that they were somehow all identical. Do you know what I mean? The manuscripts, like mannequins, lacked edge.

Like the young woman on the street whose pancake and eye shadow you want to wipe off, because you can tell she's more beautiful than that. Or pictures that hang in convention hotels. They're the right colors for the room; they project the desired atmosphere; they remind guests of great paintings. But they're interchangeable, so it doesn't matter who did them.

When you think about it, composing poems as if craft is enough, which is what I think these people were (subconsciously, I'm sure) doing, is just as evasive as hiding behind subject matter. A poet who is fundamentally a craftsperson sets out to make a beautiful object, and in the process he or she may perform superlatively—but underneath all that skill no one's home.

CLEVERNESS

Elevating style over substance does have its advantages, though. I can think of several quite famous poets who see it as a winning game. You can be recognized as an artist because you're incontrovertibly good at what you do. At the same time, you don't have to go out on any emotional limbs. There are two variations on this theme: the person who creates a gorgeously clear poem, the outcome of which is predictable but so well done you can't help but admire it, and the person who creates the exotic object, the kind of poetry that leads many readers, including literati who ought to know better, to conclude that if they, as bright people, don't understand it, then it follows that it must be brilliant. Some of these people seem to have it all: the most reviews, the best readings, the most prestigious publications, the most sought-after teaching jobs. But my guess is that the work of intellectually, but also emotionally, committed poets who are now low on the horizon, but steady, will survive them.

INVISIBLE BRUSHSTROKES

Anyhow, back to craft. You could argue that no poetry that approaches bone—the zero that Emily Dickinson was talking about—can be exactly perfect, because somewhere the hand of the maker has to show or the tension, the energy, the snap of the work is lost. Let me give you an example of this. A few years ago, a friend of mine and her husband had a house built on the outskirts of, let's say, Nashville. In the course of finishing the inside, they hired a cabinet-maker to custom-build some furniture for their daughter's bedroom—a loft, a bed, dressers, and so on. When he finished, they told him to sand the wood to a shine and paint everything white. The husband then inspected the room with a magnifying glass, and when he did, he saw brushstrokes on the furniture, which hadn't been visible to the naked eye. So he made the cabinet-maker sand off all the paint and do it again. This time there were no brushstrokes, and guess what? The result looks exactly like plastic.

There are whole magazines of this ilk around, full of the perfectly crafted poem into which the poet has succeeded, Houdini-like, in disappearing completely. That this has happened isn't really surprising. It all comes down to human nature. When we're young, most of us worry about what people will think if we stick out, so we work hard, aiming to please. Even the few who start out as rebels, trying to sound like no one else, draw such negative feedback that all but a tiny minority develop protective coloration. It was no accident that the species that survived were for the most part the ones that blended. To avoid predators, look like everyone else. The only trouble is, if you do that, no one will remember you, not even yourself.

THE JANE DOE POEM

Let's look at this from another perspective. A policeman finds a corpse in the woods. The tips of the corpse's fingers have been worn away, and all its teeth are gone, so the policeman can't identify the body. All he can say is white female, forty- to fifty-years old, tinselly hair, five-foot-eight, a hundred-and-twenty pounds. That could fit hundreds, maybe thousands of people. Do you want to be among the unidentified dead?

Do you want to be a John or Jane Doe? Of course you don't. And how do you avoid it? You take chances. When you're afraid of something you've done, far from destroying it, you go out and mine the vein.

DO WHAT YOU FEAR

When I was young, as I told you, whenever I was writing in my own voice, I was careful to present myself sweetly. But now, not. I'd rather not expose this dark side, but I know that if I hold back, then I'm putting myself forward falsely. I'm lying, and the older I get the more determined I am not to lie. Also, and relatedly, the older I get, the more I trust the words that visit me. It's a little like being led around blindfolded. There could be a cliff two steps from here. But I have to take that chance, because taking it is what my whole life is about. Besides, words are my seeing-eye dogs. They have always rescued me before, so I trust them now.

Speaking of doing what you fear, though, I have to make a confession, and this harks back to what we were talking about in the out-loud chapter. I'm one of you. Every time I get up to do a reading, I'm afraid people will laugh at me, especially at my terminal earnestness. I really don't think I'd care if they didn't like me personally, as long as they relate to what I write, since when it comes right down to it, my poems are more me than I am.

Because of all this, doing readings makes me really nervous. But I go ahead and do them anyway, because I believe in poetry—not mine, everyone's—the way some people believe in money. I think it has everything to offer us, whether we think of ourselves as "poetry people" or not. If I really mean what I've just said, then I have the obligation to stand up and say so. If I didn't, it would be like finding a cure for cancer and not telling anyone.

Be Yourself No Matter What

So here I am, and here you are, too, if you decide to go the risky route. Of course, you absolutely don't have to do that, but if you're going to set yourself up for failure anyway, why not do it right? Think about it. Suppose your poetry career succeeded beyond the most insane of your dreams. Suppose they sold your books at newsstands and in airport bookshops. Suppose you won the Nobel. Suppose you were recognized on the street. Okay, we know that doesn't happen, at least not in this country, but we're dreaming, so let it ride. Suppose you knew that when you died you'd rate an obituary in *The New York Times* and tributes on *NPR*.

Now let's further suppose that you, after all this, knew in your heart that your poetry had in fact cost you very little, and that even in the best of it, you weren't really there. Then what? Did you really set out to live the life of some anonymous person you don't even know? Of course you didn't. So how did you get here? You let fear rule you. You didn't risk.

RISK: THE BOTTOM LINE

Risk is the third rail, the bottom line. The only way to be truly yourself in your work is to risk it all. If you do that, you will in time break through your craft problems. Clouds that seemed impenetrable will clear. You'll find you can make the sun so strong that sometimes your reader will be momentarily blinded, and the benefits of your risking everything go far beyond the moment, because a great poem sets up a connection between the writer and the reader that has nothing to do with time or space. Poets who died long ago are finding soulmates now. So what is risk? Immortality.

You'll know when you're risking when your skin says, "Go back." When it says, "Beyond this place there be dragons." When it says, "This is the end of the map, do you want to die?" It's the very jolt that tells you to run, which is a sure sign you should go on. Because adrenaline is your body's response to that odd rubbery smell that tells you you're nearing the startle in which you suddenly see clearly what you never saw before. And those few seconds are what keep us writing, because they're the seconds of our lives in which we are most alive. They are, dear coffee companion, why we came.

EXERCISES
Taking Chances

Do these exercises in the first person. Don't hold back. You always have the option of keeping them private.

1. All of us have done something we've never told anyone, because we know it would make us look a way we wouldn't want to be seen. Write a poem using the most telling information you've been hiding.

2. Think of what would embarrass you the most if someone said it to you. Start with that sentence and ramble on in that voice for a page.

3. Write about your most failed sexual relationship.

4. Write about something bad you saw as a child when you were powerless to intervene.

5. Write a poem about something you, as an adult, should have stopped but instead let pass.

6. Write the poem that would most threaten your mother/brother/ sister/partner.

CHAPTER
11
READING

WHY HEAVY READING IS NECESSARY

If I had to tell you in a single sentence what you can do to write well, or if you're already writing well, to do it even better, that sentence would contain only one word: Read. Reading has enormous practical benefits for any writer. For one thing, by showing you what's been done, it will save you from dissipating your poetic energy by trying to reinvent the wheel. Furthermore, unless you do read, it will be almost impossible for you to tell what's fresh in your own work and what, on the other hand, may be limp.

Speaking of fresh, reading's an unparalleled way to keep dazzle in your life. Other people's inventiveness—their worlds, their ways of using words—can leave you wonder-struck. It can also give you ideas. On days when I don't have an ongoing project, I'll browse in a stack of books until I find myself lingering over some almost-subliminally-flickering image, and when its silver or red stars arc out from my wand and I sense little heats falling back on my hand, I know what to do: find a keyboard. In other words, reading, besides being a daily source of pleasure, can often at least get me started on the days I begin thinking, "I'll never write again."

ON IMITATION

When you're a beginner at anything—and I've mentioned this before—imitating will help you hone your skill. My 30-something-year-old singer-songwriter son, for instance, spent the years from twelve until about twenty-four doing this. But when you're past that beginner stage, I think you should avoid your literary soul-mates when you're looking for inspiration and instead seek out writers whose poetry is nothing like yours. If you stick to the unfamiliar, you're less likely to walk inside and produce a clone of what you already know about yourself. It's like living in a town in which everyone is exactly like you. If you never go anywhere else, in one sense you'll be poor all your life no matter how much money you have. Besides, all good poetry is the result of sideways motion, and people who write from worlds far away from yours (physically or psychically, doesn't matter) can expand your mind into corners you didn't know you had.

ON MUSIC

Besides exposure and inspiration, which I've just discussed, another critical reason to read a lot if you're interested in doing any writing yourself is that reading is ear training. I really believe that no one who doesn't read extensively can write fine poetry. That's because poetry is, besides being a way to convey emotions, a kind of music, and how can you hope to write music if you never listen to any?

Reading is why heavy readers who begin to write poems as adults, even late adults, having never written a word in their lives, can make sometimes astonishingly fast progress. They've internalized the way imagery works, and also the cadences of speech are already in their heads. It's like having learned a language as a child. There are certain sounds you'll be able to reproduce—such as the aspirated "h" in Arabic, or "eu" in French—that if you'd learned the same language as an adult you might well never have gotten straight. Along the same lines, I've noticed that the undergraduate papers I get from my Computers in Modern Society students consist mostly of sentence fragments. Obviously, they don't read. If they did, they'd at least have an instinct for the principles of sentence structure.

ON WHAT REALLY MATTERS

The last reason to read lots of poetry, and this applies even if you don't write or if you've stopped writing, is that if you do, sooner or later some poem is going to change you, and the more this happens, the richer you'll get in the kind of currency that matters. For instance, every time I see a snake I think of Emily Dickinson's narrow fellow, and I can never not think "zero at the bone" when I'm truly afraid. Robert Hayden's "Those Winter Sundays," which describes how an inarticulate father expresses himself to his son, has changed forever the way I understand love. You'll find that your signifying poems (and which poems those are will be a matter of who *you* are) can make your arm twang as if you were thwacking a baseball out of the park. But unless you've hit lots and lots of balls, or turned lots of pages, you may never know how that feels.

When I was teaching at the University of Florida, I used to put a poem on my office door and make my students read it before I'd help them with their programs. The morning this particular accounting major came to office hours, it happened to be "Those Winter Sundays." He had a printout of his program, due the next day, tucked under his arm. He sat down in my visitor's chair and I said, "Okay, let's see your listing." But he just stared. So I said, "You know, Matt, I really do need to see what you're doing if you want me to help you," and he said, "Well, that was why I came, but I just read the poem on your door." I said, "It's a good poem, isn't it?" and he said, "Yes," and that he didn't want help with the program any more, he was going to drive down to Tampa now (two and-a-half hours away) to visit his father's grave. And he did. I always wished I could have told Robert Hayden, who wrote that poem, about Matt, but by the time it happened, he was long dead. Maybe somehow he knew.

No matter what, if you want to write, you need to read lots of modern poetry. This doesn't mean you should ignore the centuries that came before. If you like Gibran or Sappho or Shakespeare, by all means read them (I'm going to talk specifically about that in a minute), but like it or not, most of the time you're going to be writing in a contemporary voice, so the moderns have to be part of your ear training. You may not be reading much contemporary work now, because, outside of your own poems, you think there's no one around who would speak to you. Maybe the poetry in *The New Yorker* has caused you to come to the conclusion that most modern poetry is boring or obscure or both. Or maybe you didn't like the dead white male poets you had to read in school. Here's the thing about what you read in school, though, and this may not have occurred to you—you don't have to like it. There's no law that just because someone is skilled at something, he/she will resonate with you personally. Think about it. If you were in a room with 100 acknowledged great poets, if you were in a room with any hundred people, how many of them would turn out to be your soul-mates? Two, three?

HOW TO FIND NEW POETS

To find your ideal poet-matches may take some looking, and the overwhelming number of books you'll find just aren't you. The truth is that even those of us who read poems voraciously have been exposed only to a tiny corner of the poetry universe. One problem is that there's a lot out there, but the real and deeper problem is that what's out there is scattered. Still, if you don't read much now because you haven't liked what you've seen, I can promise you this: there is a poet or poets who will speak to you. If you're already reading lots of poetry, here's an alternative statement: there are poets you've never heard of who will make a difference in your life.

So, how do you find those people? Well, one way to start is to look through some anthologies. You can begin with Norton or one of the Oxford books of verse, but you should also look at others. Thumb through a few in a good bookstore or library, or on the web, then use the contributors' notes of the poets who strike you to find more of their work.

But just reading anthologies by itself won't cover the waterfront, and here's why. First of all, the content of the bigger anthologies tends to be politically driven. The anthologized poets' writing teachers edited the books, or the editors are the friends, lovers, etc., of the included poets. For another, any anthology naturally reflects the tastes of its editors, and those tastes may or may not be yours.

The reason I'm telling you all this is that if I'd relied on anthologies—which was how I started out—I'd have missed out on some poets whose work I just love. So, you may be thinking, if these people are all that great, why aren't they in the collections? Well, there are several reasons. They may not have the right connections; they may not hear about anthologies being put together. Sometimes, they're passed over because the anthology editors happened to be biased against their writing styles.

The good news is that it's not as needle-in-a-haystack as you might think to find unanthologized poets. Many of them will have published books, so you can begin your expedition by exploring the poetry shelves in as big a library as you can find. To get started, look up the call numbers for poets you've heard of or you know you like. Look up several, because some will be shelved by the Dewey Decimal System—around 811.5—and others by Library of Congress numbers—those will be all over the map. Then go to the stacks where those poets live and see what strikes you.

Alternatively, you can look through the current issues of literary magazines in your library until you find someone who draws you. Then look that person up and see what he/she has published. I'm suggesting shelf searches for both books and magazines, because they let you physically browse, but at least when it comes to magazines, you'll probably be able to do effective searches only if you live in a big city or near a university, because most public libraries can't afford to subscribe to a broad enough selection to be useful. In that case, and even additionally, you can browse the web. Most libraries have web access, so Internet searching is practical even if you don't have a computer.

A word about the net: be sure to start with a magazine title or some other limiting word. Typing "poem" or "poetry" in naked is pretty useless because along with the results that are worth pursuing you'll get every blog and MySpace posting in the world. A good, and high-quality Internet source of new poets is *Poetry Daily,* which you can ask to e-mail you a poem every day. A lot of poets I know have *PD* set up as their home page. But don't confuse *Poetry Daily* (poems.com) with poetry.com, which is essentially a vanity site, meaning there's not much editorial control on what's posted there.

Another good thing to do on the net is to look up someone whose work you like on Amazon.com and see what the people who bought that person's books also bought.

On Prizes

When I started reading seriously, I thought that any book that had won a literary prize, especially a Pulitzer, must be the cream of the crop. Since then, I've learned that not only are prizes naturally limited ,because they reflect the taste of whoever judged the contest in a given year, but also that sometimes they're not about the work so much as the connections of the poets. There's another factor, too. I didn't know this until I'd been around quite a while, but the Pulitzer, even in years it's awarded on a level playing field, is sometimes given more in recognition of lifetime achievement than for the book that ostensibly wins it. In other words, be wary of the face value of Pulitzers (this can apply to others of the big prizes as well) if the winner is past a certain age. If he/she is, then be sure to check out the earlier books before you decide on the most recent one. In any case, no matter how many prizes someone's poetry may have won, don't forget that you still have a perfect right to dislike it. So what if someone else is telling you it's deathless work? If you get faint-hearted about that, remember those 100 great poets.

What I've been telling you so far has applied mostly to 20th and 21st century poets. Don't limit your reading to those. Read dead poets too, women and men. Once you're doing it because you want to, not because you have to, you'll be amazed at how beautiful the poems are of people you faintly, like old music, remember from school.

While we're broadening your range, be sure to track down translations from poetry around the world—especially central Europe, Africa, Latin America, and Asia. This is important, because the work of writers at the fringes of, or outside, western culture can open up your perception of what language can do.

HOW TO GET THE MOST FROM READING POEMS

To be successful at music—and as I've told you more than once, for me poetry *is* music—when you're reading, you're going to want to work on your ears. One way to do this is by getting in the habit of reading out loud. This will teach you to recognize what you musically like when you hear it. Don't forget that, as I was saying when I was talking about readings, the read-out-loud-mantra applies to your own work, too. Chant it, sing it, say it. Do this over and over. Do it when you're in the car. Do it when you're running. When you get experienced at that, you'll find your ear exposing the false notes, even before your fingers see them.

All this came home to roost when I was assembling *Desire Lines,* my new and selected. I was surprised to notice that for years now I'd been saying certain poems a little differently from the way they were written, and here's why—because without my conscious intervention, my ear had corrected my musical mistakes. So when I put the poems into that book, I changed them to match what I'd been singing.

Here's a suggestion for you. To deepen what you're gaining from reading, memorize what you love. Try to build a repertoire, the way a pianist does. You'll be glad you did. For one thing, when you're telling a friend about some poem you've read, you won't have to dig around on your bookshelves. You can just say it, and you'll have it with you all the time, even when you aren't carrying anything. Think about the difference if you're an instrumentalist (which you are) between the depth of your ownership of the piece of music you've sight-read and one you've taken the time to learn.

READ MORE THAN POETRY

Almost every writing teacher will tell you that if you want to write poems, you'll need to read lots of them. But saying that tends, if only by implication, to limit you to one genre. I think that's a big mistake. Besides poetry, you should also read contemporary fiction—from writers whose use of language is close to poetry—Salman Rushdie's *The Moor's Last Sigh,* anything by Milan Kundera, Kobo Abe's *Woman in the Dunes*— to ones whose writing isn't like poetry at all—*Engineer of Human Souls* by Josef Svorecki, for instance. You should also re-read the classics you read in school all those years ago.

Don't forget plays from Shakespeare to Stoppard, because playwrights understand compression. And don't overlook nonfiction, either. Nonfiction's especially good, because it enlarges your arsenal of facts—which you want to be as large and varied as it can possibly be since it's the idiosyncrasy of what you know that will distinguish your writing from other people's. If your only language is the one we all use, then you could be anyone. But if you write about love in, say, the language of knitting or jet engine mechanics, then your work can come alive in a way only you can make it.

BESIDES READING

Take classes—celestial navigation, meteorology, botany. Go to art galleries and museums, watch dance, try to feel the way a cat runs, spend a few hours on what's happening in the patch of grass at the foot of your chair. Listen to the slithering madrigals of Gesualdo, the ones he wrote after he killed his wife and her lover. Think about translating each of these experiences into your own vocabulary—kitchen-speak, garage-speak, pool-speak.

Keep your ears open when you're around people from other cultures, because stolen grammar patterns and idioms can sound astoundingly fresh in English. For instance, did you know that in Japan, when they want to say something is small, they say it's "smaller than a cat's forehead?" Doesn't that make you want to run right out and write?

Apropos of that, remember that anything that's happened to you can be grist for poetry. I had a consultation with a young man at a conference in Charleston, SC. once. I remember him as in his late 30s, a little heavy, with colorless thinning hair, which he combed across his bald spot. To sidestep the poems he'd brought, generic lyrics about sunsets and love at the beach, I asked him what he did for a living. He said he designed office cubicles. I said, "Wow. Think about what divided space means, and what happens to the people you (God) shut up in those boxes." Then I asked him what else he'd done, and he said, "Well, I used to work in a lab where my job was to kill the rats when the scientists were finished with them. My boss told me to put them in a big glass jar and add some chloroform, then screw the lid on. Then I was supposed to wait for them to die and throw the corpses away. But no matter how I shook the jar to even out the odds, there'd always be a few who'd crawl to the top over the rats who were already dead, and keep scrabbling until finally they died, too. I didn't think that was fair, so I didn't do it that way. I'd get the rats out of the jar one at a time. Then I'd slap them across the edge of the table to break their necks and throw the bodies into a wastebasket I kept beside me. I used to read while I did it—pull, slap, toss, pull, slap, toss. I got so good I didn't even have to look up. I just reached my hand into that jar, and got me another rat."

I said, "That's incredible. Write it down." He was astonished to think anyone would be interested. I assured him they would. It's a good story, right? Well, somewhere inside you have a story just as compelling as that one, and all you have to do to access it is to let yourself ramble. If you do that, it's bound to rise to the surface sooner or later. Why? Because stories worth hearing are survivors.

I wish I could read all the poem/stories you'll write out of all this. I know how rich they're going to be—reflecting all the reading you'll have done, of course, but even more strongly shining like lamps in the evening from what you know of your own life. Which brings me to how grateful I wake up for all the poets and novelists I've loved but never met, and how lucky we all are that we'll never, no matter how long we live, exhaust the streak we've tapped into with our little hammers ,because the vein goes on forever, deeper into that mountain.

EXERCISES
Expanding Your Repertoire

1. Set aside at least one four-hour block for each of the next four weeks for poetry fishing trips. If you have an extensive collection of books, you might spend one week on that, one week browsing the shelves in a library, one week on the Internet, and one week picking your two favorite new collections of poems and reading them very slowly.

2. Pick a craft, occupation or sport that interests you. Find some books on it and take a lot of notes. Look it up on the Internet. Be sure to include specialized publications, such as magazines, in your reading.

3. Memorize a poem a week for each of the next four weeks. At the end, say all four of them in a row out loud. Bring at least one of them up in conversation during the month.

4. Look up the list of the last twenty years' Pulitzer, Nobel, and Booker prize awardees. Read something by each of four authors. These can be poetry or fiction and must be people you've never read before.

5. Look up four of your favorite poets on Amazon.com. Look at the "also bought" list and find in the library, or purchase, at least two of those poets' books.

6. Do the same for four novelists whose work you love.

7. Read at least three "best of" anthologies from last year. These might include one one-of-a-kind volume, the Pushcart Prize anthology, and an anthology from one other series—maybe *The Yearbook of Poetry and American Verse*. Find four poets whose work you like. Find books by two of them and read them.

EPILOGUE

Now that the waitress has cleared our table and is turning out the lights, and now that I've said what I came to say, let me tell you why I wrote this book. I did it for one reason: to be useful. And I'm hoping one of the ways *Feathers* can serve you is as a friend. Someone who understands, without you saying a word, why you spend so much time on something that, even if you do it radiantly, presents no opportunity for you ever to be a "success."

When I was starting out, I would have loved to have had a mentor to help me to think more clearly poetically. Beyond the work itself, there were times I found the practicalities of the poetry scene difficult to fathom, and I'd have welcomed some older sister advice about publishing, studying, finding new poets, and all the other things I've been talking about with you.

It's not that I was living on the moon. I was reading lots of poetry and poetry texts (there are some good ones) and from time to time I also bought how-to books. But in the end, I found the texts and how-tos missing something: texts, because their approach was essentially academic; how-tos, because theirs was strictly practical. What they were missing, from my point of view, was heart. The fact is that the point of writing poems is neither academic nor an exercise in fill-in-the-blanks. Whether you write only for yourself, or you write for your family and friends, or you write for the world, the point of writing is a life point, and none of the books talked about that. So that's a gap that, among other gaps, I've tried to fill in our time together.

You see, if you live a poetic life, then inanimate things will start coming alive. If you don't like the way they're acting, you'll develop the poetic power to turn them into something else. That power, and the fact that, once you get good at seeing, what you see in any given thing will be different from what anyone else sees in that same thing will make it all worthwhile. Remember those students who went out and photographed the same grasses?

Think how great it's going to be when you finally approach being able to bring everything you've read, everything that happened to you as a child, the moment years ago when your raft overturned and you thought you were drowning—in other words, your whole existence to this point—to bear on the world that is around you right now.

I heard a story once about a man who woke up one morning and discovered, as he punched down his alarm, that for forty years he'd been living someone else's life. If you pay close attention, if you're brave enough to approach the edge of sentimentality and tough enough not to fall off, if you involve yourself in poetry so passionately you find yourself mining every detail of your life, you will never be that man.

I've loved the time we've spent together in these pages, and I'll be thinking of you as you surprise yourself, day after day, year after year. I'd like to leave you with this, like grace before a meal. Welcome, poet, to the world where forks and spoons are in love, where your dearest daughter may be a warm stone. As I write these words, I have the sense that one day I'll look out my window and that set of wings I see in the distance will be you, soaring.

LaVergne, TN USA
22 July 2010
190477LV00002B/5/A